# HUSTLING WITH HUBRIS

When Making A Deal Is Paramount

RICHARD E. TOMLINSON

ISBN-13: 9781492779292
ISBN-10: 1492779296
Library of Congress Control Number: 2013917720
CreateSpace Independent Publishing Platform
North Charleston, South Carolina

This Book Is Dedicated To:

Judge Carl Horn III, for your immeasurable support, encouragement, and friendship

My family and friends who never lost faith

Mark DeCastrique for your editorial support

Jim Dickson, Gordon Murphy, and Bill Tudor who insisted I write this book

# CHAPTER 1

THE FOLLOWING IS a true story, as unbelievable as it may seem. It represents only a few years of my life, but make no mistake, they were major life-changing years. The places I traveled to, the people I met, the chances I took, and the ultimate repercussions and consequences they had on me are simply unforgettable. There are many lessons to be learned, both in business and in life. Some joys, and some lifetime scars. Since we cannot turn back the clock, we must live with our decisions. That's just what I am doing, but oh what a ride!

In early 1986, I was approached by a friend with whom I had been involved in creating and developing a community charitable tennis tournament. The event took a year to plan and execute, and starred big names at that time—Rod Laver and Vitas Geruleutis. It was a very successful event, raising over $20,000 for my favorite charity, Developmentally Disabled.

My friend, John, was a partner in the newly formed securities firm the Pinnacle Group in Charlotte, North Carolina. He and three other senior officers from a major Wall Street firm had combined their considerable resources in an effort to revolutionize the securities industry. They quickly hired one hundred of the top-producing brokers from various firms, and opened offices in four states. The only key operative they were missing was an investment banker.

Because I had bought, sold, managed, and resurrected several businesses, he asked if I would consider joining them, as a partner, and filling this role. At first, I was reluctant, saying I had no Wall Street contacts, nor experience at raising investment capital. However, they were simply looking for someone who could put together the very popular tax shelters of the day, along with help to seek and execute small acquisitions and mergers. Feeling confident with these parameters, I plunked down the requisite $50,000 partner fee, and officially became their vice president of investment banking.

Even as a young child, I had strong motivations to succeed. I was born in my doctor's office in Dearborn, Michigan, in October 1941, which was six weeks before the Japanese bombed Pearl Harbor and the United States entered World War II. We literally lived in a converted garage. My parents were hardworking, blue-collar folks. My mom came down from the Upper Peninsula of Michigan, where her immigrant parents labored in the copper mines, along with thousands of other Slovenians who had escaped the four-hundred-year-old war of their homeland.

My father, a barber, came to the Detroit area from the red-clay farming area of central Georgia in search of making more than twenty-five cents per haircut. He eventually started his own shop, and reminded us three children of the old adage, "If I'm worth a dollar to you, I'm worth two to myself." I never forgot it.

At eight years old, I was already making money, cutting grass, shoveling snow, growing a garden, and finally selling newspapers on the street corners. I saved enough money to purchase my first bike, and at age ten secured my first paper route, delivering the *Detroit News* to sixty customers seven days a week. The money was good, and I was off and running with my first taste of financial independence and entrepreneurship.

Through my teen years, even though I played three sports, with emphasis on football, I was regularly employed. I cleaned butcher blocks in a meat store, sold women and children's shoes, drove a furniture-delivery truck, and some summers worked in the car factories during model changeover, scrubbing concrete floors with an acid powder to clean up the previous model year's embedded debris. I always had money in my pocket, helping to generate a very independent attitude.

Finally, when it was time to go away to college, I was fortunate to have been offered several full-ride football scholarships, and I accepted the one at Arizona State University. Near the end of a great freshman year, I reinjured my knee, and that was the end of my football career. I transferred to Michigan State University, and immediately needed to figure out a way to pay for the next three years. Fortunately, I decided to try my hand at my first independent venture, and started University TV Rentals, supplying students, primarily coeds, with a portable TV set to view their favorite soap operas and sports programs.

I had virtually no money to purchase capital equipment, and had read in the paper that two men had lost a contract to supply the area hospitals with rental TVs in each of the patients' rooms. The deal I cut with them was that I would take sixty of their TVs, rent them out, and split the proceeds fifty-fifty on a pure revenue-sharing basis, which worked out great. I paid the rest of my college and living expenses with this business, and was even able to sell it upon my graduation. The taste of entrepreneurship was delicious, and ultimately I would be searching for more, much more.

# Chapter 2

Immediately prior to the Pinnacle Group opportunity, I had spent almost twenty years doing what interested and challenged me. This included working for Ford Motor Company as a zone manager, and overseeing groups of Ford dealers. I was fascinated by their business and survival skills, particularly during a sixty-nine-day strike by the UAW in 1968. By now, with a wife and four children, I needed a serious increase in income, and was lured to a local television station to sell advertising time, graduating to national sales, management, and being the VP general manager of a major TV station, all within the space of four years. I quadrupled my income within the first two years of entering the broadcast industry. During a hiatus from broadcasting, I obtained licenses for the sale of securities, insurance products, options, and finally real estate. Returning to broadcasting, but this time as an entrepreneur, I sought out and purchased several radio stations that were either bankrupt or badly underperforming. Resurrecting them was great fun, and I quickly sold them for a profit, generally within a one-year period.

It was these activities and experiences that interested the Pinnacle Group partners to ask me to join them. Previously, while I was licensed in securities, I learned about tax-sheltered programs, which included real estate, gas and oil, and cattle. The federal and state governments had offered to either defray, delay, or limit taxes on investments in these areas in an effort to encourage capital to flow into them and help stimulate the economy. Today, some people challenge such tax breaks as "loopholes," and are angry because they exist. The fact is that the tax-sheltered programs were available to anyone and everyone who wished to invest, and literally brought hundreds of millions of dollars into needed sectors of our economy. (An example would be an investment in Section 8 housing, a federal government program that incentivized private capital to build and own multifamily properties for low-income citizens).

Therefore, over the next several months, I created one real estate investment program, working with local general partners, called MedCenter Inns, which had the unique marketing target of buying motels/hotels that were in close proximity to hospitals. Families were encouraged to stay in these facilities, sometimes for extended periods of time, while a family member or loved one was undergoing medical treatment.

My biggest success came after one of our brokers introduced me to the president of an area trucking firm, referred to as an LTL carrier (less than truckload). I worked for six months completing exhaustive due diligence and putting together a marketing package to take to Wall Street, as investors there were the only ones who had the ability to raise the approximately $55 million that was necessary to grow the firm.

I went to Wall Street and literally went door to door, cold-calling on all the big boys—Morgan Stanley, Goldman Sachs, Merrill Lynch, and DLJ (Donaldson, Lufkin, Jenrette). Interestingly, when I got into the lobby of Goldman, the man I had an appointment with greeted me, put his hand in my face, and said, "What do you mean bringing me a deal this small. Go away and don't come back until you bring me a one-hundred-million-dollar deal or more"! Here I was in my finest blue striped suit and silk tie, and he went about three hundred pounds, had no coat, his tie was undone, his shirt unbuttoned, and sweat poured from the top of his bald head. The lobby was full of other capital seekers like me, and although I was embarrassed, I was far from discouraged. So much for confidentiality. I had heard Goldman had a lot of class; I just didn't know it was all third!

Shortly after this introduction to "the big boys," I was ushered into the offices of DLJ. The company had an analyst who had followed the career of the CEO that I was marketing, and he was most anxious to hear the story. Ultimately, we made a great deal, with DLJ assisting with the venture capital (initial seed money so the trucking firm could start a new division), then mezzanine financing for working capital to help with the daily growth (intermediate financing), and finally an IPO (initial public offering) to raise money from the public to dramatically expand the rapidly growing company. It was an exciting and great learning experience, being co-manager of an IPO with a first-class Wall Street firm, and we weren't even a full year old at the time. The six-figure commission check I earned for the firm was more than any of the professional brokers had generated.

Meanwhile, as the trucking deal proceeded toward a successful conclusion, we were approached by the largest Black Angus cattle rancher in the United States and asked if we were interested in participating with him in developing some tax-sheltered cattle programs. He had done many in the past, all successfully, and was simply looking to expand the marketing reach of his Brentwood Farms, located in Brentwood, Tennessee. Overall, his story was rather compelling. He had ranches in four states, ran approximately eleven thousand head, owned some national champion bulls, and managed the complete cycle of impregnation, gestation, and safe and healthy delivery with his skilled team of veterinarians and support personnel. A key asset, he represented, was the fact Brentwood had twenty-five thousand straws of prize frozen bull semen in a refrigerated vault that could be used for artificial insemination should the opportunity present itself with other willing buyers, either locally or anywhere in the world. He had completed many such investments through a local broker-dealer, so the track record he presented had credibility. His name was Gary Rose.

The investment concept was actually pretty simple. Investors would purchase a cow from Brentwood, it would be impregnated by one of the rancher's champion bulls, and a progeny would be the result. Because of the tax-shelter program, the investor could write off the feeding and keeping of the mother, and ultimately the offspring would represent the profit. It could then be kept until maturity, and procreate as well, or be sold to another willing investor or buyer.

Visiting the primary facility in Brentwood was indeed very impressive. The main office was in a magnificent, old southern-style structure the owners affectionately referred to as Tara, with its tall, white towering pillars, easily viewed from the distant driveway entrance. All around were white fences, with roaming Black Angus cattle grazing lazily as far as the eye could see. Investors were brought to the farm to get a first-hand view of what their investment would look like. The rancher knew exactly how to get folks excited. Generally, the visitors were all men, and the ranch hands would arrange to bring in a cow in heat, followed very closely and aggressively by a bull looking for an afternoon delight. Once the bull mounted the cow, cheering broke out. I'm not sure whether the cheering was for the bull, or whether it was the result of the investors' being able to actually see the creation of their investment literally in the making. Either way, it was a hell of a great marketing tool! My guess is that upon returning home that evening from this business trip, the men's wives and/or girlfriends were met by a rather amorous mate.

Back at the office in Charlotte, the rancher made his final pitch for us to create several tax-sheltered investment products and begin marketing and raising money. Included in the meeting was the manager of the securities firm's insurance products. He indicated that the cattle program would be the perfect product in the insurance portfolios of his clients, since most had cash available in the Whole Life policies, and the cattle program was projected to return an average of 12 percent per annum. He indicated that his father, who was a representative of the same insurance company, would participate as well, and had literally thousands of clients that counted on his advice and counsel. Therefore, the die was cast, and the first three tax-sheltered cattle investment programs came to fruition, money was raised, and within a relatively short period of time, profits were on the horizon.

# CHAPTER 3

In early 1988, I received a phone call from the rancher, requesting an urgent meeting with him and his corporate attorney. They flew to Charlotte, and four of us, including the insurance broker, met off-site. They explained that the Tax Reform Act of 1986 was eliminating tax shelters involving cattle, and that this would cause a loss of revenue for the huge ranch operations and even threaten some of the existing investment packages we had put together. The **answer** was simple. They claimed that since the Black Angus carcass yielded far more usable and preferred meat than any other breed, the cattle in and of themselves had more value. However, the **real** value was in the exporting of breed herds to Europe, where the animals, as well as the prize bull semen, would fetch double the price per pound they did in the United States. The attorney presented the plan. They would create a partnership between them and me, whereupon I would go to Europe and meet with the requisite governmental officials, sell them on the idea, and begin exporting huge numbers of the animals, along with the "how to expertise." Knowing full well that this would take many months, if not a year or two to complete, the attorney turned to the insurance broker for the immediate funding of the ranches and the overseas program.

As the attorney described it, the rancher would personally issue promissory notes, in his name, collateralized by the assets of the ranches, namely (and primarily), the thousands of animals themselves, along with the frozen straws of semen. The notes would bear anywhere from 10–14 percent interest, depending upon what it took to raise money from the insurance clientele. He further shared his professional opinion that there was nothing illegal with these transactions, since "any private citizen is allowed to borrow money from other private citizens, if they both agree to the terms." Initially, I was very wary of his advice, as I was licensed in securities, insurance, and options transactions, and some of what he said flew in the face of my understanding of securities laws. He assured me that there were no violations of securities law, state or federal, so I ultimately acquiesced to his interpretation and his experience in practicing law for many years. Finally, they presented a certified financial statement, with the balance sheet showing over $10 million in assets, all owned by the rancher personally. The financials were issued by an "independent" CPA, who regularly kept the books. A new partnership was formed, and I left the Pinnacle Group.

Before I left for Europe, the rancher and his attorney had another pending opportunity that needed attention. The rancher had been contacted by a medical doctor in Jamaica who wanted a partner in a special project. As it turned out, there were two deserted dairy-processing plants on the island, because the lack of refrigeration throughout the country made it insufficient to support an ongoing business. Instead, he had perfected a process called aseptic packaging, wherein the milk would be inserted into these sealed, sterilized bags and sold through local markets. The main advantage, of course, was that these milk packages had a shelf life of six months, as opposed to spoiling rather quickly in the heat, without refrigeration.

The rancher and I flew to Kingston and met with the doctor. Over the next several days, we toured the entire island in his four-wheel-drive vehicle, rumbling along miles and miles of rough country roads, visiting the defunct dairies, passing through areas of abject poverty, and generally getting the lay of the land to determine where we would place and breed the cattle. After extracting the milk, we needed to set up a completely new operation to package and distribute the milk products.

The projected cost of taking over the dairies and rehabilitating them, as well as attending to our own operational needs, was one million US dollars. Even though this project had nothing to do with the European program, it seemed to me to be yet one more major opportunity to expand into international markets, creating a larger footprint for our newly formed relationship, and one that had a major profit potential since we would be in complete control of all milk distribution in all of Jamaica.

An all-out effort was launched to raise the money, and finally when we had the commitment from a source, the investor made it contingent upon a firm contract with the Jamaican government, which owned the dairies and the land. Also, we had to have a majority position in the agreement.

After several meetings with high-level officials, we were told that the Jamaican government would be the majority owner, and the government had written a very lopsided contract in its favor. The end result: we had to walk away from the deal.

Therefore, it was time for me to make preparations to go to Europe, with the first stop being a meeting with the lord mayor of London.

# CHAPTER 4

As my plane was about to land at London's Gatwick Airport at 6:20 a.m. London time, I realized I was close to being brain-dead. I cannot sleep on an airplane, and losing five hours because of the time difference meant I was entering into another workday, essentially with no sleep. After deplaning and going through customs, I headed straight for the Gatwick Hilton, located inside the South Terminal of the airport. I was able to collapse in a fresh queen-size bed, long enough to regain some semblance of mental clarity before heading for the Gatwick Express, the rail line that connected to the center city. From the Victoria Station in London, I took a "black cab" directly to City Hall for my visit with the lord mayor of London. Fortunately, this little amount of shut-eye was sufficient for my first day in London, and allowed me at least a modicum of alertness in this important meeting.

Once admitted through security, I was immediately summoned into a magnificent room, very Victorian, and the lord mayor himself was awaiting my arrival. After exchanging pleasantries, he asked if I would like tea, and was promptly served by a uniformed assistant, on a very expensive-looking silver tray. The paintings displayed on the surrounding walls must have dated back centuries, along with the ornate chandeliers. I felt I had stepped back a couple of hundred years in time, and was essentially mesmerized by the beauty and elegance of it all. However, we got right down to business, as the lord mayor had many questions as to exactly what it was that I was seeking, as well as the background of my company, the cattle rancher's history, and my personal bona fides.

My primary objective, I shared with him, was to essentially replace the entire United Kingdom's herd of breeding cattle, since it was now commonly known that they suffered greatly from "mad cow" disease, or more formally, bovine spongiform encephalopathy. At this point in time, there had been no proof that the disease, which was killing their animals, was transferrable to humans. Still, the export of British beef, particularly to Europe, had significantly decreased. I offered to replace their herd with our superior breed of Black Angus, which were not only healthy and much more marketable, but had more usable meat per animal. He was fascinated by the suggestion, as well as by the opportunity to see what the next steps would be. At this point, I requested that he put me in touch with the import/export minister for the United Kingdom, and he obliged.

Later that afternoon, I had a previously arranged meeting at the London headquarters of the Bank of Credit and Commerce International, BCCI. The bank was coming on very strong internationally, being very aggressive in all areas of financing, but in particular providing financing for agricultural endeavors. The bank was founded in 1972 by a powerful Pakistani named Agha Hasan Abedi. It had grown rapidly, including in the United States, through the acquisition of existing banks. The bank wanted the legitimacy and connections that successful banks had built up over the years. However, within the year, there were rumblings about BCCI's being involved with billions in money laundering, particularly in working closely with the Medellin Cartel. More on this later.

The bank had come to my attention while I was in New York meeting with one of the largest agricultural lenders in the world. Rabobank, an international financial institution headquartered in the Netherlands, was also founded in 1972. I was seeking a partner for our European venture, by either an injection of equity or at least a loan of several million dollars to ensure the successful accomplishment of our strategic plan. While the bank's representatives were very courteous and professional, ultimately they turned me down, citing the fact that virtually all the collateral we were offering at the ranches was "on the hoof," live animals. They said that too many things can happen that would jeopardize their investment with us, not the least of which was the animals' coming down with a disease. Believe it or not, their second objection had to do with the security of the herd spread out over four states—yes, they were worried about cattle rustling! At this point, they suggested I meet with the BCCI folks, as they had already gained a reputation for being extremely aggressive.

Back in London, I entered the plush offices of BCCI and was directed to an anteroom, just outside a large conference room. In short order, the gentleman I had contacted to set up the meeting appeared and ushered me into the conference room. I wore my best (and only) blue, pinstriped "banker's suit," along with a shirt I had purchased on London's famous Jermyn Street, and a rather snazzy silk tie, and it seemed like a long way for a kid who was born in a garage earlier years earlier!

Upon entering the room, briefcase in hand, and a presentation safely filed in individual folders for the participants, I extended my hand in greeting, "Hi, I'm Dick Tomlinson," whereupon the first gentlemen, taking my hand, said, "Oh, hello, Rich-aard," (Richard with his British accent). The next, and the next, and the next greeted me in the same fashion, after I had said my name was Dick Tomlinson. The meeting progressed, with me presenting all my wares and asking for a three-million-dollar loan. After a two-hour meeting, with many relevant questions asked and responded to it came to a conclusion. Before we officially adjourned, they promised they would give serious thought to my proposal, and get back to me within two weeks.

However, as the men filed out of the room, I took my contact aside and asked him to explain what I considered a rather strange phenomenon. I said that my recollection of the British was that they were the quintessentially proper, cultured people. I was perplexed, however, that when I shared my greeting by announcing my name, Dick Tomlinson, each had responded, essentially correcting me, by calling me "Rich-aarrd." His reply to me first stunned me, and then I howled with laughter. He said, "Surely, Richard, you must understand that in Britain a "dick" is a body part!" Point made, case dismissed! I was "Richard" for the rest of my European travels.

Before returning to the United States, a British official introduced me to a Hungarian attaché, who was named Joe Blasko. I had no idea at the time that this man would completely change my world, and the direction of all my efforts.

# CHAPTER 5

THE NEXT DAY, I returned to my office in Charlotte, where I had a suite of three rooms, and one employee, an office manager/bookkeeper/secretary. Florence was about sixty years old, had tons of experience in the areas I needed support in, and was perfectly happy working by herself during all my extended absences.

The operational structure I had set up with Gary, the rancher, and the two insurance brokers who were by now soliciting full time for funds to support the rapidly decreasing revenue stream was that since the brokers were both based in North Carolina, they would bring in the signed notes and accompanying checks to my office and give them to Florence, who would then deposit them in our corporate account at NationsBank (now Bank of America). The funds would then be wired, within twenty-four hours, to Brentwood, Tennessee, and placed in the rancher's bank account. Once a record of the notes and their respective owners was recorded in my office, they were mailed to Gary Rose in Brentwood.

I was surprised at the high level of success the insurance brokers were having, and already within approximately the first six months, they had raised over a million dollars. On a monthly basis, I would receive a financial statement from the rancher's CPA, and even though times were getting somewhat more challenging, the numbers always appeared solid and did not raise any specific concerns by me.

I had two specific, demanding goals: create an ongoing, structured, profitable enterprise in Europe, and in as many countries as possible; and, second, simultaneously meet with major prospective global banks in an effort to bridge the interim period between when the new Tax Reform Act seriously impinged upon the operating capabilities of the four ranches and the point at which I had an agreement in Europe, shipped the cattle, and received the cash. Time was not on our side, but it appeared that the monies coming in from the insurance brokers would be sufficient until I could close a deal. Unfortunately, sometimes we get ahead of ourselves, and even though some puffy white clouds were appearing on the horizon, none appeared to be dark, and certainly not stormy, or so I thought.

# CHAPTER 6

"YOU'VE GOT TO come to Budapest right away," Blasko insisted. "We need your cattle and expertise far more than the Brits do, and I have all the contacts you will ever need to get the job done. We are desperate here, and you will be handsomely rewarded for your efforts."

During the 1980s, Budapest, and all of Hungary, was still occupied by troops of the Soviet Union. Hungary was a key participant in the ongoing "Commie Con" marketing structure that the Soviets had set up after WWII. The "market" consisted of about eleven countries, including Czechoslovakia, Romania, Yugoslavia, and several others, along with Hungary. The system was set up and dictated by the Soviets, as to what crops would be grown, what livestock would be raised, and by whom. Hungary's primary contribution was agriculture, featuring its famous paprika, but also cereals, sunflower seeds, pigs, and cattle. The entire system was set up on a barter basis. With so many disparate currencies, with high volatility daily, barter was the most reliable method for evaluating and exchanging goods. Hungary was the only net exporter in the entire group. It was not until 1990 that Mikhail Gorbachev, president of the Soviet Union, decided not only to tear down the infamous Berlin Wall but also to enact reforms that eventually led to the collapse of the USSR, freeing countries such as Hungary to begin life anew, as independent, free entities.

On my initial trip to Budapest, Rose and I had a layover and plane change in Frankfurt, Germany. Once again, we arrived very early in the morning and quickly found an area full of benches in the enormous Frankfurt Main Airport. I grabbed a cup of coffee and checked on the departure of my next flight, on Malev Airlines, the official airline of Hungary. Sitting down, the gentleman next to me struck up a conversation, asking what I did for a living, and where I was going. Happily, I shared with him that I hoped to regenerate huge beef herds throughout Europe, particularly in the Eastern Bloc countries that had been severely impacted by the long Soviet occupation and adverse influences.

At the end of the thirty-minute chat, another gentleman who had apparently been sleeping on the bench across from us sat up and stared at us for a moment. He was unshaven, with somewhat rumpled clothes. He interrupted, and said "Excuse me, but I couldn't help but to overhear your conversation. Do you have any plans in going to Croatia?" No, I said, I hadn't thought about it. He then said that he would very much like to introduce my program there, as well as in several other countries in the area. He then handed me his card and left to get some coffee. On his card, it simply said: Rudy Perpich, Governor of Minnesota!

My introduction to Malev Airlines was rather stark. The seats looked and felt like they were lawn chairs bolted onto the floor. Once airborne, most of the passengers lit up cigarettes, and soon the cabin was filled with the most acrid, eye-watering sensation I had ever experienced. Most Eastern European cigarettes, even though they had American brand names like Marlboro, were unfiltered and had local tobacco, which was much, much stronger. Wow, the flight was almost two hours; how was I going to survive this atmospheric onslaught? About thirty minutes into the flight, an attendant came and asked if I would like a "snack." Starved, I said I would appreciate one, and soon she delivered to me what the Hungarians refer to as a snack. I lifted the lid, and in the middle of the plate was a whole roasted Cornish game hen! Vegetables and multigrain, fresh-made bread surrounded the bird. With everyone eating, the smoke cleared, and the meal was simply outstanding. I found this to be just a small sampling of what I would find during the many months I spent in both Budapest and the surrounding countryside.

# CHAPTER 7

WE ARRIVED IN Budapest, Gary Rose, the rancher, and I, on a gray, chilly afternoon. Upon the plane touching down, we were escorted to the gate by two armed vehicles, one on each side of the aircraft. At first, we were concerned, thinking that someone on board was being sought after for criminal activities. However, we soon realized that the whole of Europe was on alert for terrorist activity. In fact, while we were in the Frankfurt Main airport, armed guards with automatic weapons patrolled everywhere in the terminal.

The taxi trip to our hotel was an interesting experience. First, the vehicle seemed to be made of cardboard, as the fenders were cracked, and instead of seeing bent metal, there were layers of fiber, with pieces missing. These were the old smoke-spewing diesels that the USSR had legislated into all its subservient neighbors. The billboards were fascinating, since we couldn't make out the Hungarian language, but could easily see the products being advertised. The term "Magyar" was everywhere, referring to an ethnic group associated with the Hungarian people.

We had been preregistered in a hotel by Mr. Blasko, the Hungarian contact we had met in London. The locals called it...the "Rah-Mah-Dah," which of course we found out was a Ramada Inn! However, it was no ordinary American version of the motel chain. This facility, located on Margaret Island, in the middle of the beautiful Danube River, had been one of the city's famous health spas for almost a hundred years. Built with approximately two-foot-thick walls of solid stone, and featuring a huge hot bath as its centerpiece, where people from all over the world came for aquatic therapies, it was truly a masterpiece. While awaiting the arrival of Mr. Blasko, we enjoyed taking advantage of our new environment.

At 6:00 a.m. the next morning, with jogging shorts on, I hit the path along the Danube for a five-mile run. Much to my surprise, I passed a long stretch of clay tennis courts that were already teeming with young people blasting away at the fuzzy yellow balls, to the shouts of multiple instructors. Since I was an active tennis player in the States, I watched closely the incredible level of skills these young folks had developed. My thoughts ran to these thirteen-to-eighteen-year-olds soon to be seen on the world stage of tennis greats.

One other special treat I received while jogging was the sunrise over the famous Hungarian Parliament building, and glistening off the Danube, as well. Simply breathtaking. On my way back to the hotel, I noticed a modest, solid-stone church that was dated from 1100 AD. I couldn't believe my eyes, at the realization that literally billions of people have lived and died since it was constructed, and it survived ten centuries of wars, famines, and everything else we humans could think of to destroy humanity…and religion. Two days later, I attended a Catholic Mass at the church, not understanding the priest's homily, but fully understanding the prayers and procedures of the Mass itself.

The day after our arrival, Mr. Blasko showed up at about 11:00 a.m., and our indoctrination to doing business in Hungary was about to begin.

# CHAPTER 8

Mr. Blasko advised us that he had set up meetings with very important people in the Hungarian government, with whom we would be able to conduct business both officially and unofficially, and that the meetings would begin the next morning. Therefore, he suggested, we enjoy a Hungarian liqueur, Unicum. Unicum has been a Hungarian staple for decades. Brewed by the Zwack family with a secret formula of some forty ingredients, it is somewhat thicker than an ordinary liqueur, and is semisweet, with a unique flavor all to its self—and enough power to knock your socks off!

After about three hours of this social extravaganza, and hoping we drained the hotel's supply of Unicum, we finally sat down to have lunch. Hungarian meals are liberally served with baskets full of six or eight different whole-grain breads, along with slices of meat, cheeses, and sausages. Adding a bowl of homemade goulash, we were ready for a nap by midafternoon.

# CHAPTER 9

THE NEXT MORNING, a car was sent for us, and we were transported into the center city of Buda, where all the government buildings were located. Pest, the other half of Budapest, is located across the Danube River. Our first appointment was with Mr. Lazlo Kapoli, the minister of commerce for Hungary. He was an older, very distinguished gentleman, well dressed, and able to speak a form of "Hungarian-English." Since neither Gary, my partner, nor I spoke any Hungarian, we were able to communicate by listening very carefully and digesting what we thought we heard before responding. The meeting between Blasko, Kapoli, and us lasted about two hours. However, a critical foundation was laid by the commerce minister, allowing us to better understand exactly what the realities were for how to operate in Hungary, legally and logistically. After understanding exactly what we had to offer, an operational blueprint was sketched out so that everyone knew the role each was to play.

Mr. Kapoli explained that we had to have a partner who was Hungarian. This was typical of many countries around the world, and we were somewhat surprised, but delighted, when he suggested that partner should be himself. As well, he further added that we would need a key governmental player to assist with bringing all the animals, equipment, semen straws, and necessary vet medicines into the country, and offered a friend of his, the import/export minister for Hungary. We were now getting a more comprehensive understanding of how things were going to work, and couldn't think of better partners than these two key ministers.

Mr. Kapoli then shared his vision of the other key contacts that would be necessary to put our adventurous plan in gear. First, we needed to meet with the officials at the Bank of Hungary and get them on board for the financing support that was envisioned to complete the various transactions. Next, he said he would set up a meeting with the officials at the University of Hungary's Veterinarian Department, since they would be instrumental in assisting with all the necessary inspections, shots, and artificial inseminations that would take place shortly after the cattle had arrived from the United States. Finally, we would need to meet with the managers of the largest farm co-op in the country, a sixty-thousand-hectare layout (equal to 148,000 acres) with three thousand employees, resting just north of the Romanian border. This is the location where all our Black Angus would ultimately be located for breeding and feeding purposes. They would be flown into Budapest on a 747 that we had pre-arranged, with specific interior structural improvements to protect the animals during the long flight.

Over the next several days, the meetings with the bank officials and university personnel basically went as planned. There was a cautionary sign, however, when meeting with the bank. Through our interpreter, we learned that the bank would be very cautious (no surprise here) and require a great deal of paperwork ahead of time. However, we realized, too, that the official currency of Hungary was the Forint, which was very volatile, not universally accepted, and prone to serious inflationary pressures. Unbeknownst to us, this would be a critical, potentially fatal roadblock in the future. However, since I owned 55 percent of the company formed by Rose and I, and by all estimates this was going to be about a $22 million deal, I wasn't about to let a $12 million payday slip by so quickly.

That evening, a rare treat was in store for us. We were invited to a special reception at the Hungarian Parliament by the EBRD, the European Bank for Reconstruction and Development. This bank was similar to the World Bank, in that it was funded by dozens of nations around the world, including the United States, and its goal was to inject either equity or debt or both into worthwhile enterprises in the Eastern European bloc countries, which had been decimated by World War II and had not sufficiently recovered, even with the help of the Marshall Plan. In Europe, this was referred to as merchant banking, and at the time was illegal in the Unites States, but now it is legal. During this reception, I was given a personal introduction to the president of Hungary, and had a brief but very meaningful discussion with him, and he pledged any and all support we needed to be successful in his country.

After procuring a very competent lawyer who spoke both languages fluently and constructing the necessary contracts with the various parties, we prepared for our first trip 160 kilometers south, to the huge and beautiful co-op, Mezeheges.

However, the weekend was upon us, and Blasko invited us to his sister's house for what he referred to as a luncheon that afternoon. We arrived at the small, cinderblock house, in a rather impoverished-looking area. We did note that there were several old, beat-up cars out front. Upon entering the home, we were received by his sister, who rushed across the room and gave us all a big hug. Then, further to our surprise, lined up against the wall were about fifteen to eighteen people, including children, who, we were told, were family members. They all stared at us Americans while they sat on very old stuffed chairs, including some metal folding chairs.

We were ushered into the kitchen, and were absolutely astounded. I've never seen so much prepared food in one place in my life. Blasko's sister had prepared at least a couple of dozen Hungarian specialties: meat dishes, breads, fruit, vegetables (some of which we didn't even recognize), soups, goulash(s), baked goods, fish (fogosh, a local pike), and of course many cheeses. But first, we were brought back into the living room, where now everyone was standing. The sister handed us fruit-juice glasses filled with the family's own homemade brandy, and with a loud "egga shegga," everyone slammed down the first of about a dozen toasts. Oh my God, were we going to survive this incredible hospitality? Three hours later, my body simply could not take another bite of food or drink. I would have thought seriously of offering to trade my first-born child for a two-hour nap, but fortunately was able to stay awake and socialize as best we could, considering the severe language barrier. Never have I met more loving, thoughtful, and generous people. Blasko told me I couldn't offer his sister money—that would insult her. So I sent a large basket of flowers to her, and was told she was so proud of it, since she had never received one from a florist before, that she marched around the neighborhood showing it off!

# CHAPTER 10

AFTER SPENDING SEVERAL weeks in Hungary, it was now late fall, 1989, and during the evening, an early snow began to coat the landscape. Our driver picked us up promptly at 5:00 a.m. in Mercedes sedan. Unfortunately, he spoke no English whatsoever, so we knew the roughly three-hour trip was going to be a long one, but we had no idea the adventures we would encounter.

About fifty kilometers outside the city, the snow came down even more heavily. Of the two major highways that provide for rapid transportation in Hungary, ours went north and south, and like the other highway, it was only three lanes—the middle of which was for vehicles to pass whenever they felt the need, and whichever direction they were going. Essentially, you play the famous game of "chicken" every time you pass, hoping an oncoming vehicle, using the passing lane as well, will ultimately tuck back in and allow you the right of way.

The Russians were still in evidence throughout the country, and never more so than on the highways in the countryside. As we were making our way through the snow-covered landscape, we looked up and saw one of the enormous Russian military trucks in the center lane passing other vehicles. It was obvious that there wasn't enough room for both of us, and as the truck approached, our driver dove to the right and landed us in a ditch about three feet deep, full of snow, ice, and water. The driver was frantic, and we were stuck. So I got out of the car, waded into the ditch, motioned to the driver to get back in the driver's seat, and with my suit, tie, and leather wingtip shoes on, proceeded to push the vehicle back onto the road. Later, through an interpreter, the driver begged us not to tell the story for fear he would lose his job. We agreed.

Another hour down the road, with conditions continuing to worsen, the driver pulled into a small farmyard and parked next to a house near the barn. We learned later that Mr. Kapoli had prearranged for us to stop at this smaller co-op so that we could get a sense of what we would find at the much larger one down the road. The experience was one of a lifetime.

As we entered the home, a woman greeted us in Hungarian. Our driver responded, but we had no idea what was said. She very politely ushered us into the kitchen, and provided us with fresh bread, cookies, and cake. Within a few minutes, two huge Hungarian farmers, brothers, entered the kitchen in their overalls and extended their hands in a greeting. Their handshake was like a vise, and their hands literally wrapped around mine and my partner's. At this point, they sat down, and we all realized we couldn't understand each other. So, spotting a large tablet of blank paper, I put it on the table and began to play…"Pictionary"! I can't tell you how ridiculous my attempt at drawing a cow and a bull was, but somehow they got the message (it was the utter hanging underneath that did the trick). I had considered drawing them mating, which was at the very core of our program, but decided that may be pushing our nascent relationship just a tad too fast! They then drew pictures of sunflower plants and paprika fields, which somehow made sense.

At this point, the brothers decided we were friends and asked their sister to bring in a half gallon of homemade brandy, a staple in Hungary. Now, it was 8:00 a.m., and they were pouring juice glasses full of what seemed ultimately to be 200-proof breakfast juice. Each of the brothers lifted his glass in a salute, pronounced "egga shegga," to our health, and slammed down the whole glassful! Not only was it early morning, and we had not eaten breakfast yet, but my partner was Southern Baptist and virtually never drank alcohol. As the brothers put down their empty glasses, they stared at us, so to avoid being disrespectful, I downed my brandy, too. Then with eyes on my partner, who was just sitting there, I told him this is one hit he has to take for the team. He raised the glass, took down the liquid in about three separate gulps, gasping all the way, and within ten minutes was totally unconscious, sleeping in his chair!

Then, a wonderful surprise happened. The sister walked into the room with another lady, who greeted us in English and said she was requested to come and assist the four of us. Over the next hour, we accomplished a great deal in understanding how the farm worked, what the co-op members' needs were, what role the Russians played, and the time frame for these intruders to return to their native Soviet Union. The pricing of crops and the pedigree of their animals was all information that would be helpful to us on our next visit. As we began to depart, and I woke my partner from his unbridled stupor, I asked the lady where she had come from at the last moment to save our visit. She smiled and asked us to walk out into the front yard, snow and all. Pointing across the street, we saw an elementary school, with a couple of dozen children's noses pressed against the frosted window panes, trying to get a glimpse of the American visitors. As it turned out, she was the only teacher at the school, and upon hearing from her sister about the dilemma across the street, volunteered to come help out. We found this so wonderfully typical of all the Hungarians we met during our travels.

# CHAPTER 11

AFTER ONE MORE hour on the road, dodging the oncoming Russian monster trucks, we arrived at Mezeheges. The huge sixty-thousand-hectare complex, lying among the somewhat desolate countryside, was littered with barns, fences, small out-buildings, where they kept farm implements, residential facilities for the three thousand employees, and a magnificent primary facility with commercial-size kitchens, dining halls, and stone fireplaces that rose ten feet above the ground floor. The fireplaces were big enough to hang and roast deer and other wild animals that were regularly killed on the property. Unlike many of the smaller farms in Hungary that still used mules and horses to pull their plows, this operation was fully mechanized, since it was a primary provider of beef, pigs, and many seed crops that were used for the country's bartering with other Soviet satellite countries.

The president of the co-op and several of his management team greeted us warmly, and soon we sat down to talk business. They wanted detailed information as to our breeding operations, size of the current herds, proof of the quality Black Angus we were promoting, details on carcass reclamation (that is, how much usable meat could be delivered from an average-size cow of "x" weight), bona fides of the national champion bulls, and their respective frozen semen straws, diet of the animals, history of diseases, current immunizations, shipping procedures and costs, and the timing of delivery. They were aware that all the financial details would be worked out between the Hungarian government and us, so that was not an issue for discussion.

Together with the additional visitors from the University of Hungary's vet school, we took a two-hour tour of the massive facilities to determine what their capacity for additional herd stock would be, where they slaughtered the animals, where the artificial insemination was to take place, and the extensive laboratory network they had to support such an operation. Everything was very impressive, and one look at the pathetic beef herd they had, with ribs showing, and overall just scrawny animals, it was obvious why they were so eager to do business with us.

Finally, it was dinner time, and we were welcomed into the upper chamber of the main facility, which was a beautifully rustic dining room, with pine walls, and an enormous oak, handmade dining table that accommodated about twenty-six of us, and that smoky aroma that had accumulated on and into the wooden walls from the fireplaces over the past century. Naturally, they started with about five toasts, with their version of homemade brandy, and I thought I'd have to put a net under my partner so that when he fell and hit the floor, he wouldn't hurt himself! Wisely, he faked throwing down the drinks and survived.

Next, we were served a large bowl of ox soup, rich with a brown broth, fresh vegetables, and meat. Unfortunately, I bit into a small piece of bone and broke off a molar at the gumline! Further, I wasn't due back into the United States for another three days, so it was all grin and bear it. The main course was all from their land. Freshly killed venison, pheasant, and wild boar topped the main course. Fortunately for the brandy, I was able to enjoy the entire meal without having my dental problem interfere. Then it was bedtime, and we were put up in relatively small rooms, impeccably clean, again with all rustic, homemade furniture and a working fireplace.

The next morning, I heard noises outside my door, which opened to the out-of-doors. When I opened the door, I was shocked to find five or six area businesspeople lined up to speak with me. Word had gotten out that there was an American businessman in the area, with money to spend, who was looking for opportunities to invest in local businesses. As well, there was an interpreter standing ready to help. Needless to say, I didn't want to be rude to such wonderfully hospitable people, and who knew, there may be additional values to be had. In actuality, the folks were trying to sell old sewing-machine manufacturing facilities, farm-implement stores, and other miscellaneous businesses that simply didn't fit with our game plan.

So it was back on the road to Budapest, to catch a plane back to the United States the next day. What awaited me would change the course of the entire endeavor, and sooner than I had thought.

# CHAPTER 12

AFTER WE LANDED back in Charlotte, North Carolina, my partner and I went to my office and called the two insurance agents to join us, giving us an update on their capital-raising efforts. The news was not particularly good, but it didn't seem to be a major problem at the time. By now, the four Black Angus ranches were relying heavily on the insurance brokers' generating sufficient funds through the sale of promissory notes to keep their doors open, primarily because the Tax Reform Act of 1986 eliminated the financial benefits to all investors, so their investible funds found other products. The costs of operating the ranches continued to rise, but the price of beef in the United States was declining, which was the primary purpose of looking to more lucrative markets, particularly in Europe. Gary Rose, my partner, encouraged the insurance brokers to continue doing all they could, and assured all of us that the collateral he had shown originally on the balance sheet almost a year ago was still accurate. However, it was obvious that additional major efforts needed to be pursued in order to raise sufficient capital to bridge the time gap until we could clear all the import and financial hurdles required to successfully undertake such a massive transfer of livestock.

On a previous trip to Brentwood, Gary and I went to one of his favorite delis to have lunch. Once inside, we ran into one of his better-known Country and Western star investors, Larry Gatlin. I wasn't privy to the conversation they had, but Gatlin was decidedly upset with Gary. Later, Gary told me it had to do with a debt he owed Gatlin. Gary also had clients such as The Judds, Waylon Jennings, among other famous names.

Then, during one of my trips home in December, I received a rather frantic call from Gary's wife. She said Gary had had an accident and was in the hospital. She said that their long, winding driveway had become very slick during a recent ice storm, and that he had slipped and fallen, all the way to the street level. I flew to Nashville and visited him in the hospital. He was in such bad shape I could hardly recognize him. One side of his face was wiped out, with all the skin gone. His shoulder was incapacitated with a torn rotator cuff, and his arm and leg had bones broken in three places. He couldn't have been in worse shape if he had been dropped from an airplane at five thousand feet. I never did buy his story of sliding down the icy driveway, and to this day believe someone beat him up. Someone he had done wrong, most likely in the finance or cattle-breeding business.

Gary's CFO in Tennessee had put the word out that they were in search of a major loan, to the tune of several million dollars, which would be supported by the ranches. The late eighties was a time in the United States when hundreds of cons were operating, very successfully, and living off people looking to raise money that had a marginal balance sheet (ours being primarily of live animals, which no bank would touch). In a short time, it seemed people literally came out of the proverbial woodwork, offering to do business with us. There was always a catch, however. Every one of them required an up-front fee, usually, $50,000.

The offers came from St. Louis, where a reinsurance company offered to provide additional collateral in the form of a reinsurance policy, from a British firm offering the same product, from a Miami investor from Iran, and finally from an investment-banking firm in Panama. Being somewhat naïve as to all these private sources, and sensing that my partner wasn't necessarily telling me the complete truth about the ranch financing, I began to pursue all offers. The most aggressive, and seemingly the most promising, was the firm in Panama. It gave us references in the United States, whom we contacted and who seemed credible. As well, the firm promised it could do a limited stock offering utilizing our assets (cattle) and raise several million dollars. This put them at the top of the list, and a trip to Panama was soon planned.

I invited an attorney friend of mine, who had been on the staff of the Securities and Exchange Commission in Washington, DC, to accompany me. We landed in Panama City, and were immediately put into a holding room, without any explanation. After about an hour of being detained, I requested to speak with the head of the investment bank who had invited us. Ten minutes later, not only were we released, but a car came to whisk us away into the city, and a meeting where the principals of the firm were awaiting our arrival. They presented multiple documents showing they had the capability and capacity to raise significant amounts of capital throughout the world, not just in the States. They had our documents preliminarily prepared, and offered us a list of area attorneys who specialized in these types of financial transactions. We chose the first one listed, a woman, who had excellent credentials, and was available that afternoon.

After more due diligence on both our parts, we tendered a check for $50,000 and went to lunch. The restaurant was an outdoor, festive setting, and we chatted with our attorney and ate the special of the day, a warm chicken salad, with area nuts and fruits mixed in. Then it was a return to the United States, with promises that our monies would be raised and in our bank within the next two weeks. The day after we arrived back in Charlotte, I became very ill, and all my skin began peeling off, as if I had some kind of leprosy. My attorney from DC had eaten the same thing I did and had gotten ill on the plane ride home. Ahh, nothing like a little food poisoning, which apparently turned out to be much less than the ultimate outcome of our visit, where we gained what we thought was access to badly needed capital. Upon arriving at the Panama City Airport, while waiting in line to board the flight back to the United States, I was approached by a machine-gun-toting soldier who pointed at my watch, and said: "Nice watch." I thanked him and turned away, whereupon he grabbed my shoulder and repeated what initially I thought was a compliment. At that point, I got pissed and simply walked through the open door to the tarmac, and stood at the base of the plane awaiting boarding. I looked over my shoulder and saw him staring at me. I boarded the plane immediately.

During the next two weeks, I called frequently to the firm in Panama, only to speak to an associate, who told me the principals were working on raising the capital and were not available. Finally, I had had enough and decided to return to Panama. I booked an airline ticket and a hotel near the airport in Panama for the next day. Then I received a phone call that stunned me. I was in my office at five thirty that evening when the phone rang. A voice on the other end said he would not reveal who he was, but that he was calling from Washington, DC, and that he saw on the records that I had applied for and received a visa to travel to Panama the next day. The voice warned me NOT to travel, because there was going to be "action taken by the US military that may endanger my safety." What? I couldn't believe what I was hearing.

This was the time when former president Jimmy Carter had offered to go to Panama and help oversee the presidential elections. Manuel Noriega was known to be very involved with the drug trade, and the US government wanted him badly, since most of those drugs were entering this country. As it turns out, Noriega was also utilizing BCCI, the bank whose representatives I had met with in London, to launder his funds.

I cancelled my plans based on whatever credibility this mysterious phone caller had generated with me. It was December 1989. The next morning, I awoke to the headline news that the United States had just invaded Panama, and saw the news footage of where one of our gunships had fired into the side of a hotel, the exact one I had been booked into. "Operation Just Cause" was fully under way, and thank God, I was safely at home in Charlotte. To this day, I have no idea who was behind that phone call, but if you read this, may God bless you!

Within a month, a headline in the *Wall Street Journal* stated that this "investment banking" firm with which I had been dealing was internationally known. The principals were being arrested, and to further my naiveté, listed among those being sought was my Panamanian lawyer, **who was married to the CEO of the fraudulent firm!** Talk about a slick con game, this was hard to beat. That $50,000 good-faith deposit we had made disappeared faster than Noriega's reputation as an altar boy did!

Next, I flew back to London to meet with the reinsurance company executives that had made contact with us. I went to their offices in the financial section of the city, was greeted by their receptionist, and about fifteen minutes later was shown into their conference room. I met with two principals of the company, and they explained exactly how the reinsurance business works, and how it could provide the additional collateral support we would need to bolster our balance sheet, and raise the requisite capital to proceed with our plans. The office was a very busy place, with people coming and going, and after a two-hour meeting, I left feeling comfortable with the results of this meeting. They asked for a check for $50,000, and I told them I would return in a couple of days with the funds. They were most insistent that they would not begin the procedure until the funds were in their hands. I returned three days later to consummate the deal, and when I approached the building, I was once again shocked. The place was completely empty, with no signs of life anywhere. They had apparently rented the place for just a few days, did all their dirty work, and vanished without trace.

I contacted Scotland Yard, and its officers said that since no crime had been committed, they would not pursue the matter. However, they put me onto three ex-Scotland Yard detectives in private practice, and shared my story. They were intrigued, and about a month later informed me that they had tracked the perpetrators, and that they were members of an international crime syndicate that was flourishing.

Meantime, it was time to return to Hungary and finalize all our plans and commitments, and hopefully get the first 747 full of cattle in the air as soon as possible.

# CHAPTER 13

My MEETING WITH representatives of the Bank of Hungary did not go as I had hoped. They could not guarantee their support of the effort for multiple reasons, the volatile Forint being one problem, the use of live animals as collateral, not knowing what the market would bear once the breeding herd was in place, and so on. In other words, for some reason, actual or political, they dumped out.

I met with my Hungarian partners and shared this news with them. They told me that they had an alternative, and they would share it with me over dinner the next evening. When we met at a wonderful small family-owned restaurant in Budapest, there were two other persons present. They were introduced as governmental officials from the Ukraine. It was said that they would provide solutions to two problems. First, they would be excellent customers for the breeding herds we were about to develop. Next, and this was the key, since the multiple currencies of the United States, and the Eastern European countries were the biggest problem, they suggested we go back to the barter system that had worked over there for so many years, and was so successful.

The deal would work like this. We ship the cattle to them, they in turn ship hardwood timber, in equal value, to us, and we sell the timber through prearranged contracts to buyers anywhere in the world. We get our money, they get their Black Angus. Seems simple enough. Seeing a light at the end of the tunnel, I phoned back to my partner in Tennessee to tell him the good news, and to start preparing for the first load to be

RICHARD E. TOMLINSON

sent within a month, as the Ukrainians said they could have the timber within a week.

One small problem arose on the phone call. The sheriff answered the phone, saying my partner had split with whatever remaining money there was in the till, the authorities couldn't find him, and most of the cattle had been sold off months ago. The year 1990 was not shaping up to be my favorite year.

— 46 —

# CHAPTER 14

THE FLIGHT BACK to Charlotte took nine hours, and I don't remember it at all. I was too stunned at the news, and I simply couldn't comprehend the impact of what I had just been told.

After landing, I went to the office to check with my office manager, to corroborate the sheriff's statements. She concurred. I booked the next flight to Nashville to meet with the authorities, who by now included a court-appointed trustee.

At the ranch in Brentwood, they shared all the sordid details of my partner's last several months. Yes, he and his CPA had been cooking the books for over a year. Cash flow had diminished monthly, and the insurance brokers had run out of clients who would part with their spare cash, even at the now heightened interest rate of 16 percent. Worse of all, Gary had been selling the cattle, slowly but surely, over the past year to generate operating funds. Equally as offensive was the fact that I was told the prize national bull semen supply never existed as frozen straws in storage.

What had begun with the best of intentions was in a disastrous heap. There were enough truisms, such as that the Black Angus cattle were a superior breed, allowing more usable meat off the carcass than other breeds. And, yes, the ranches were real, as well as the original breeding herds. What my now ex-partner hadn't planned on was it would take about three years to put the entire European project together, and no matter how he and his CPA got creative, they weren't able to pay the bills. His exit was to avoid having the note holders come after him, not to mention the civil and criminal authorities.

As the authorities and I sat and discussed the remnants of the ranch operations, the trustee, much to my surprise, proposed one last-gasp effort to make the note holders whole. He asked me if he could round up enough Black Angus from other area suppliers, could I still make good on the contract with the Hungarians? The trustee had some background in expensive livestock, being a breeder of sophisticated Arabian horses. I commented that the contract was still valid, and that they knew nothing of what had happened here in Tennessee. I further explained the new twist with the elimination of the purchase by currency, replaced by a barter transaction. Essentially, if they could gather at least five thousand head of cattle and some prize breeding bulls, I would see what could be done to gather the timber and convert it into cash.

The desperation, survival plan was agreed to, and all I had to do now was to find someone who was expert in timber quality, quantity, and global contracts! I was given a very short leash by the trustee and sheriff of about one week to come up with a viable plan, and two more weeks thereafter to execute the plan. Whether it was a case of hubris, or just because I had put in several years of very hard and creative work, I never doubted that I could pull the proverbial rabbit out of the hat yet one more time. I was driven primarily by the fact that it would be unimaginable if the promissory-note investors would lose all their money. But now, to say the least, time was of the essence.

# CHAPTER 15

I HAD AN old friend in Chicago with whom I had done some securities business, and who had been with the Chicago Board of Trade. I called and explained my dilemma. Immediately, he put me in touch with an experienced commodities trader, and we agreed to meet within the next couple of days.

The trader met me in my Charlotte office, and he immediately understood the need. However, he explained the facts of life to me, as it related to the best way to package timber to make it most salable. He said we would need commitments for three hardwoods: maple, oak, and mahogany. The Ukrainians had said they had the first two, but even with my limited knowledge, I knew full well that mahogany didn't grow where eight feet of snow fell every year. Where, I asked my new colleague, were we going to find mahogany? His answer was quick: Belize. Belize!

I had to look it up on the map. And yep, there it was, with plenty of jungle, and, hopefully, a supply of mahogany that was available for harvest and sale.

However, I was getting the proverbial cart before the horse. I asked the commodities trader how I would know what quality we were getting from the Ukrainians and the Hungarians, and moreover, how would I value it for sale on the world market. He said the only way he knew for sure was to take a client of his with me, return to Budapest, and finalize the deal.

His client turned out to be one of the largest owners of timber in the United States, and was the quintessential good old boy who lived in a small town in Louisiana. Oh, he said, better do it quick and be careful, because he is the longest-living heart-transplant patient in this country, already having survived seven years!

# CHAPTER 16

SITTING DOWN ONE more time with the authorities in charge of liquidating the Brentwood Farm complex, I shared the game plan. I requested, however, that they at least pay for the airline portion of my trip back to Hungary, to which they agreed. Next, I called M.L. Luneau, in Louisiana, and found he had already been contacted by my commodities associate, and he simply asked, when do we go?

M. L. met me in Charlotte, and we boarded the international flight together. M.L. was in his midsixties, nicely dressed, and had a full head of hair and the most unusually smooth skin on his face and forehead. He looked as if someone had polished his face. He spoke with a strong "backwoods" southern drawl, but was educated, so his pronunciation and enunciation were clean. He was also a gentleman, and very respectful of our relationship, and the team of airline attendants that attended to our needs. He did bring one surprise, though: the foreman of one of his strips of land, a character named Bunky. Rough, swearing, uncouth, uneducated, looking like he had just had a fight with bush hog, and lost…badly. The two of them could not have been greater opposites, but as M.L. later explained to me, Bunky was the hardest-working white man in the state, and he was undyingly loyal, I was told. "Tell him to do the impossible, and he'll get it done in half the time." OK, it wasn't for me to question…as long as they could help me close the deal.

We landed in Budapest late and went straight to our hotel…briefly. First, unfortunately, there was a casino right across the street, and both

M. L. and Bunky needed a piece of that action. Much worse, and to my chagrin, Bunky had told the cab driver to wait for us. I thought we were going to catch a late dinner, but as soon as the three of us got in the cab, good old Bunky told the cab driver to take us to the nearest whorehouse! I couldn't believe my ears. However, the cabbie understood, and within ten minutes, we pulled up to a house on the edge of town, and there it was: literally, a house with a red light glaring in the night. Pardon my extraordinary naiveté, but here we were, and I was feeling like some character in a two-bit novel.

In we trek, and were immediately greeted by the madam and three other professional associates of hers. Gentlemen, please choose your pleasure, and she then proceeded to list the house ground rules. "None of this, some of that, and all of THIS that you want." Old Bunky was thunderstruck by a gal in heels that towered over him by six inches. He grabbed her by the hand, and in a Louisiana twang that she couldn't possibly understand, off to the nether world of bliss they traipsed.

This Catholic man, married with five children, not only had not been in a whorehouse before, but wasn't about to get my fire lit that night. Thought I'd just wait until I got home, and enjoy getting to know someone I already knew quite well even better!

By now, I was wondering if M.L. was going to test that seven-year-old, borrowed heart of his. After all, the man who lost his life to save M.L.'s may have not only used it for good purposes similar to this as well, but may be mighty proud he extended M.L.'s pleasure in life.

However, M.L. sat next to me, while the madam offered us a beer, in a glass. I passed on the glass and drank directly from the bottle, as did M.L.

Now, I must say, that was the first and only time in my life I sat and waited for someone to get screwed in the next room, hoping the entire episode would be over quickly. And Bunky didn't disappoint, as he was out in twenty minutes. Amen, now we can get the hell out of here and get back to the hotel for a good night's sleep.

The next morning, I convened a meeting with my Hungarian partners, the Ukrainians, our attorney, and my two guests from Louisiana. We got right down to the basics of what type of lumber they would deliver, the volume of each type, the expected valuation, and the specific source. Here is where we found out what the Russian definition of their newly found capitalism was.

Both Ukrainians said they were governmental officials, and that they had the right to clear-cut hardwood from forests around the towns they managed. When asked specifically who owned the timber, they commented: "Who cares, it's just like in America…free enterprise, right?" At this point, I knew we weren't going to get any land maps, deeds, or authentic paperwork from them, and our Hungarian attorney simply said we have a contract for them to deliver the goods to a railhead at the Hungarian border. If they get in trouble with other Russian authorities, that's their problem.

I asked M.L. if he was satisfied with the authenticity of their knowledge, and their pledge to deliver exactly what we needed to secure a load of quality timber worthy of being purchased on the global market. He said he was, and that was that.

Now, I explained to my Hungarian partners that we needed to complete one more step in the overall deal. M.L. and I had to go to Belize and find a stand of mahogany, negotiate its purchase, cut it, and make it available for delivery in our package. I had no idea what I was getting myself in for!

As a reminder, the deal was structured as follows: We supply several thousand purebred Black Angus cattle, plus prize bulls (that we purchase at market in the United States), double the price to the Europeans, and receive hardwood timber in exchange. With the mahogany, we purchase it as it stands, harvest it, package it with the Ukrainian timber, mark it up sufficiently for profit, and make the entire package of three hardwoods more marketable. The commodities broker and M.L.'s expertise would be relied upon to ensure a positive outcome with the timber.

We returned to the United States and began preparing for what turned out to be the trip of a lifetime, to the jungles of Belize, just to conclude a deal that had begun over two years prior, one that kept taking twists and turns at every step of the way, and which essentially bore little relation to the original concept. But, come hell or high water, I was determined to get it done, and to ensure the Brentwood note holders would not lose a dime. At least, that was my plan.

# Chapter 17

The planning for a trip into a jungle was not something I had learned in Business 101 at Michigan State. This jungle was raw, not the tidy well-worn paths, and riding on the backs of elephants, and staying in elevated sleeping quarters with locals doing all the cooking. No, this was expected to be the real thing.

The smartest purchase I made, as I had been warned, was Skin So Soft, sold by Avon. The potency of the product was invaluable, I had been told, to keep the huge, jungle insects from eating me alive, and in the end, no truer words had been spoken.

The commodities broker asked to join M.L. and me on our journey, to ensure the quality and quantity of the mahogany available. He also had made contact with a soldier of fortune-type renegade, who was left over when a timber company exited the jungle, and with whom he had done a fair amount of business in the past. The broker assured us that with this jungle-trained survivor, we would have an excellent guide. OK, let's have at it!

We arrived in Belize City, and took a motor vehicle (cab would be too nice a term) to a small village on the bay, close to our point of departure the next morning into the jungle. Our accommodations were comfortable, in straw-covered units, with no pavement, just sand. Fortunately, there was a real, and I mean real tiki bar just a hundred yards away, and we soon made ourselves comfortable. Ah, maybe slightly more than comfortable, as by nine o'clock, we had put away sufficient booze that would last us for a few days. I returned to my room, only to have a knock on the door about an hour later. A voice whispered that she wanted to have some company for the evening, and was sure that I did as well. I shouted back, "Go find Bunky!," and went back to sleep. Since he wasn't on this trip, I figured he would appreciate my thinking of him anyway.

The next morning, we were up at six, and on our way to rendezvous with our guide. His name was Jack, and he looked like a throwback to an early Tarzan movie, in the Johnny Weissmuller era. He was dressed with a broad-brimmed hat with a leather-strap string, khaki shirt, combat-style boots (well-worn), a thick brown leather belt around his waist, canvas pants, and most importantly, a forty-five-caliber handgun, stuck in a holster on his right side. Half-heartedly, and not really wanting to know the answer, I asked him if he ever had to use the gun. He stared at me as if I were from another planet, and responded: "Are you shitting me. I've killed as many assholes out in the jungle as I have animals." Whoops, no more questions from the prosecutor. Case dismissed.

The real joy, however, was awaiting us just behind where he was standing. His vehicle of choice, to transport the four of us, four hours deep into the jungle, was a flatbed, 1947 Ford truck, with only a chassis, an engine, a front seat, wheels, and a fuel tank. No body, no lights, no windows, nothing.

Before we took off, he explained that the timing of the trip was critical. Four hours in, one hour on foot, mark our trees, one hour back on foot to the "vehicle," and four hours' drive through the thick brush, so we could arrive before sunset. Once the sun went down, if we were still in the thick brush, we would be in trouble. "Everyone understand? Good, now M.L., you ride up here with me, and the two of you (me and the commodities broker), jump up on the flatbed, and off we go."

Yep, off we go, about one hundred yards, and the broker and I are bouncing down on the solid metal bed like a couple of crows that just stepped on 150-degree asphalt! Whoa, I said, there is no way we can survive another five minutes of this, let alone eight hours. I was already having back spasms, so something had to be done for me to tolerate what was ahead. When he stopped the truck, I saw two worn-out, discarded rubber tires lying beside the road. I went over, picked them up, threw them onto the truck bed, and the broker and I proceeded to stick our butts down into the center of the tires, and this provided us with sufficient cushioning to survive the trip.

We began the slow, bumpy ride into the outer reaches of the jungle. Initially, it was simply tall grass in all directions. Gradually, there were some small, stunted trees strewn over the landscape. The sun was brutally hot, with no clouds in the sky. The humidity was increasing by the minute, building up to the ultimate afternoon brief but torrential downpour. As we began to enter into more of what I had anticipated was a jungle, the trees increased in height, and a canopy began to form, which was welcome shading from the direct sunlight.

Fortunately, I had slathered myself with the Skin So Soft liquid, as there were insects/flying bugs that literally bounced off my face and exposed skin, rather than landing and enjoying a brief snack at my expense. Our heads were constantly turning in every direction, looking for a hungry wild beast to pounce upon us. At first, we thought this was just an exaggeration of our imagination, but we were taking no chances. Also, as the foliage thickened, there were overhanging limbs and vines everywhere, and the thought of having snakes drop down on our unprotected bodies scared the daylights out of us. Of course, Jack, the guide, was loving every minute of our discomfort.

A couple of hours into the jungle, now very thick with growth, and the sunlight virtually obliterated, we came upon what appeared to be a campfire, still smoldering. In the middle of the fire were the remnants of a rubber tire. Jack told us that if you are ever broken down and in danger in the jungle, lighting a tire on fire, which sends up a plume of black smoke that can be seen for miles around, is the universal signal for help. Good. Check that little beauty, and file it away for future use, if necessary.

After a most uncomfortable four hours, we came upon a Mayan encampment, where we stopped, and Jack was met by the apparent elder of the group. After a ten-minute conversation, Jack returned to our truck and began to explain where we were going from here. First, he said that the Mayans would lead us on foot into where the mahogany was located. We looked at the men, who were very small, about four feet, six inches, up to five feet, and they were all carrying machetes, and shotguns and rifles. I asked the dumbest question I had asked in forty years: "What are the guns for?" One of the Myans told us that there had recently been several incidents of a very large jaguar killing their cattle and pigs. Next really stupid question: "How big is the cat?" They said it measured about thirteen feet, seven body, and six tail. Oh, OK, no problem. I was just hoping these guys were good shots, but since the animal was still on the loose, they couldn't prove it by me!

So off we all trekked, with the Mayans leading the way, chopping the undergrowth, which could grow a foot a day with all the rainfall and hot temperatures.

Finally, after about forty-five minutes, they stopped, pointed up, and there they were, beautiful mahogany trees everywhere. Jack got out a can of spray paint, marked about a dozen trees, then sat down and made some entry onto a map he carried, so that he could return with the necessary equipment and manpower to fell the trees.

Now, time was of the essence. We had used up exactly half our allotted time, five hours, and needed to retrace our steps at exactly the same rate to ensure returning safely before the daylight disappeared. And, speaking of disappearing, instead of all the Mayans turning around and walking back with us, most of them simply went into the brush, and were gone. We didn't know whether they were going hunting, or had to pee. Either way, they were history. The head of the group, however, led us back to his encampment.

At this point, we shook hands, thanked him, and jumped back onto the '47 Ford flatbed truck. Jack cranked it up, and away we went, for about an hour. Then our hearts sank when the radiator began overheating and blowing out steam. With the engine too hot to operate, Jack shut it off, cursing like a sailor, or at least like a jungle man. Now what do we do? To make matters much worse, M.L. was beginning to dehydrate more quickly than the rest of us, and began to down the balance of the water we had in two jugs. He was clearly not doing well in the heat with his heart transplant, and the commodities broker was beginning to freak out.

I asked Jack what our next trick was…burning a tire? He said that someone had to go for help, and it wasn't going to be him. M.L. could barely walk, and the commodities broker was scared shitless. Now, I'm not saying there wasn't a bit of stain in my own britches, but someone had to seek help.

This now becomes one of the stupidest things you've ever read. Not knowing exactly where to go for help, and not particularly wishing to be the next menu item for the thirteen-foot jaguar, I left off on foot, but first protected myself. Yes, I had a Swiss army knife in my pocket, the smallest one made, with about a two-inch blade. I opened it, and figured my only chance was to jab it in his eye if attacked. Yes, you read that correctly. The knife did have a red handle, and I figured that if he devoured me, eventually he would poop and folks would know my ultimate fate.

I followed the tire tread we had created when entering the jungle. Fortunately, and literally with the grace of God Himself, I had walked less than a mile when came upon another Mayan encampment. When I approached, I was greeted with a language I didn't understand. So, back to my attempt at communication, I began making the sound of a roaring engine, then with my hands emulating breaking a stick, I was attempting to tell him we had broken down, and needed help. About my third attempt, with this Mayan staring at me as if he had just witnessed something he would tell his grandchildren, I heard a loud voice, with a British accent, shout: hey man, what the hell you jabbering about?

As it turned out, he was left over from a British mining company, and had worked in the jungle so long, he decided to make it his home once the parent company folded its operations. I quickly explained our dilemma, and he went and retrieved a large water can, filled it, and accompanied me back to the stricken vehicle. Pouring the water in the empty and thirsty radiator, Jack cranked it up once more, and we were on our way back.

The problem now was we had wasted about two precious hours, and Jack lamented that we would have to go to plan "B," as he had no head-lights, and we were going to miss our destination point by sundown.

With just about an hour left of daylight, but three hours from where we had entered the jungle, we came upon a hut of sorts, and Jack yelled that we hopefully lucked out. He had seen a tall antenna next to the building, and Jack emerged from the facility with a smile on his face. He advised us that the resident of the hut was a ham operator, and had the ability to make radio contact with civilization. Further, he told us he had contacted the owner of a small private landing strip that was a friend of his, had given him the coordinates of our location as best he could, and said his friend was sending a small plane to pick us up. All we had to do was find a clearing close by and get the attention of the pilot as he flew overhead searching for the four of us.

We found the opening we were looking for about a quarter mile away. It wasn't much, and the terrain was full of humps, many of which were giant anthills. Minutes ticked away, and it was getting darker and darker. Finally, we heard the roar of a small plane overhead, and we all began running around, waving our hands, and shouting (as if THAT did any good). The plane finally saw us and began to descend, making a very tricky landing by going over the tall trees, then dropping quickly onto the surface where we were standing. The plane came straight at us, bouncing and heaving, and came to a stop about ten feet in front of us.

Joyfully, we all approached the craft as the pilot flung open the door to welcome us. Looking into the cockpit, I couldn't believe my eyes. The pilot was the fourteen-year-old son of the man who owned the craft. He shouted for us to get in quickly while the propeller continued to whirl. Now, this was a four-passenger Cessna, and was about to take five grown men into the sky. OK, have at it! The pilot revved the engine, with three of us totally squashed in the back, and good old M. L. in the front seat with the pilot.

As the craft started roaring forward, the kid, I mean pilot, started slapping at a bug in the inside of the windshield. We would go intermittently airborne after hitting one of the anthills, then slam back down to the ground because of our lack of air speed. Finally, with sufficient speed, we did become airborne, just in time to see a wall of trees just yards in front of our plane. As we approached the huge trees, I instinctively raised my feet up off the floor of the craft, as if that would help us miss being lodged in the tree trunks.

Miraculously, we cleared the line of trees, literally by inches. Then by this time, it was almost pitch-black, and the pilot found his way back to dad's dirt landing strip, which was illuminated by a string of one-hundred-watt bulbs, that only the kid could see from the air. Thanks, dad, thanks son. Now, where is the nearest bar, and place to change my shorts!

After the first three minutes in the bar, which equaled three beers as well, I couldn't help wondering if this is how they teach investment banking at the Ivy League schools.

# Chapter 18

Upon returning to the States, I met one more time with the trust officer and the sheriff of Brentwood County, and shared what appeared to be very good news with them. It appeared I could get the deal done, which was worth about $22 million, and would comfortably cover any losses the note holders had experienced, and have some left over for my troubles.

The next day, I phoned the authorities in Belize City to inquire as to what needed to be done to begin harvesting the mahogany trees we had marked. They asked me to give them the exact coordinates where we expected to begin cutting.

Later that afternoon, the news arrived. The trees were located just inside the rain forest, which was protected land, and we could not proceed.

Advising all parties concerned, I got back on a plane to Charlotte and sat quietly for about five hours, dumfounded at the experiences I had just undertaken in the previous three years, only to have this result.

Little did I know, however, that the worst chapters of my life had yet to be played out.

# CHAPTER 19

ABOUT A YEAR went by, and I had no contact with my ex-partner, nor the insurance brokers. I had heard that they were sued, in civil court, and had lost. I was not part of that suit. Fortunately for the note holders, the court required Phoenix Mutual Life Insurance Company to reimburse the clients of the two brokers, who had their licenses with the company. The insurance company was cited for a failure to supervise the brokers. Over three and a half million dollars was spent by the insurance company to reconcile with the suitors, and I believe they still came up short.

Another year passed by. It was 1993, and I got a phone call that I'll never forget. "Hello, Mr. Tomlinson, I'm Jim Hart (not a real name), and I'm a special agent for the FBI. Myself, and a special agent from the IRS would like to come visit with you. Would you have time tomorrow?" With my heart pounding, and my body beginning to sweat, I asked myself, why in the world do these men want to speak with me? I phoned the corporate lawyer I had used for a great deal of my business activities and asked him to join me. The time and location of the meeting were set, and my curiosity ran rampant through a night of no sleep.

The meeting took place in my office. The two federal government officers sat down, and the conversation began.

"Mr. Tomlinson, were you partners with a Mr. Gary Rose in a cattle venture"?

Yes, I was. At this point my lawyer asked a question that **should always be asked in a situation such as this: Is my client a target of your investigation?**

**They said no, and we proceeded with the questioning.**

**This was a huge, immeasurably damaging decision. We should have requested, in writing, amnesty since they stated I was not a target. We didn't, and the consequences were life-altering.**

The two agents said they were simply trying to find Mr. Rose, and requested my assistance. I gave them the last known address and phone number I had for him, which was about two years old. They began to probe more deeply into exactly how we met, what was our business model, where did we do business, with whom, and how did we raise money and capitalize the company. Dozens more questions were asked, as they took copious notes. My lawyer and I could not see any reason for not helping in every way I could.

Then, prior to the conclusion of the meeting, they asked if I could provide them with any records of my association with Mr. Rose that would help them in their probe and ultimately have him stand trial for the damage he had done to the note holders, the façade he had put up, the false financial statements he had given to me and various banks, and ultimately his disappearing and leaving so much carnage behind.

No problem, we said, and proceeded to allow them access to the files in my office. These files, incidentally, included all the bona fide contracts I had executed with the Hungarian government, the ministers of commerce and import/export (my partners), the Bank of Hungary, the University of Hungary, and the huge co-op where we were to ship all the cattle.

CAUTION: Have you noticed there were no Miranda rights read, regarding self-incrimination? These guys were good, very, very good. They were well trained, and extraordinarily skilled at gaining your trust, extricating damaging information, smiling all the while. They then also have the privilege of recording their notes in such a way as to tell whatever story they want, in their own way. The court and prosecuting attorneys see this subjective information, but you never will.

After about two hours, the meeting adjourned and they left, thanking us warmly as they disappeared.

Four years and 364 days after the alleged criminal conduct, I received a piece of mail that brought me to my knees. It began, "The United States of America vs. Richard E. Tomlinson." The timing was such that it was one day—that's one day—short of the expiry of the statute of limitations. A friend of mine who is a federal judge told me that is how weak the government's case was—that prosecutors went one day shy of five years trying to find some way to charge me with a federal crime, along with Rose and the two insurance brokers.

My life in hell was just beginning. I was now part of the justice system of the United States of America, and, as in the Eagles record "Hotel California," once in, you are never let out.

# CHAPTER 20

I ENGAGED A criminal attorney who was highly recognized in the Charlotte community. He had represented people such as Jim Bakker, the infamous televangelist who created the PTL Television Network, and bilked hundreds of thousands of people out of tens of millions of dollars while living a very high lifestyle. I should have taken closer note, because Mr. Bakker wound up getting something like a forty-eight-year sentence in a federal prison in Minnesota (later reduced as being excessive).

I asked my new attorney about the indictment process. How was it that I was indicted on twenty-two counts of fraud, along with the other three previous associates, and I never even knew I was being charged? He laughed and said that the government has an incredible inside track here. A prosecutor can go to the sitting federal grand jury, which convenes for periods of up to six months at a time with the same jurors, and present whatever case he wishes against you, and you have no right to go in and defend yourself. It is 100 percent one-sided. Worse, over the months, the prosecutors get to be very close to many of the jurors, because they see them so often, to the point where they essentially give a rubber stamp of approval to whatever that prosecutor brings into the room. That "rubber stamp" is powerful, and unilateral!

And here is the MUCH worse scenario: 99 percent of the people who have been indicted by a federal grand jury enter into a plea agreement, or are found guilty at trial. Why? Generally, it is thought that a regular jury in a courtroom trial assumes the defendant must be guilty, because a federal jury already has passed judgment on the issues at hand. Not a bad deal for the government folks, but a horrendous outcome for the defendants.

Meantime, this criminal attorney demands $150,000 from me, up front, to represent me, saying my case unquestionably will be dismissed. If we have to go to trial, we will win. Several days later, I told him I was only able to raise $100,000, and asked if he would take the case on that basis. He agreed, saying the first thing he would do is file for a change of venue, from the federal court in Nashville to Charlotte, where I lived and did all my business.

We flew to Nashville, appeared in court, and the judge said no to the change in venue, ruling that since the rancher was the nucleus of the criminal activities, the proceedings would stay in Tennessee. At that, my lawyer said I needed to get an attorney licensed in Tennessee, and departed on the next plane back to North Carolina. I had known him for three weeks, he had done no representation for me, pissed off the prosecuting attorney initially by saying he had no case and we would fight it and win, then kept my $100,000 deposit and I never saw him again!

Now, you are hopefully getting a taste of our criminal justice system in action, from BOTH sides of the fight, with you in the middle.

# CHAPTER 21

An OUTSTANDING ATTORNEY named Peter, in Nashville, was selected, and I can't say enough not only about his skills and experience (he had been a prosecutor himself, and now was a defense attorney), but about him as a person. He was (and still is) the best.

Shortly thereafter, a meeting was scheduled in Nashville with the assistant district attorney who was prosecuting this case, the FBI special agent, my new attorney, and me. They explained to me that I had two choices, and two only. First, go to trial, and they guaranteed I would be convicted, and spend eight and a half years in a federal prison. If I would save the government the time and expense by plea-bargaining, it would let me off with only three years, and they gave me about ten minutes to think about it. PRISON OR PRISON. THOSE WERE MY TWO CHOICES? They went on to share the statistic I mentioned earlier, that 99 percent of people indicted by a federal grand jury are found guilty. The twenty-two charges prosecutors brought against me were a standard, prepackaged litany that they use in the majority of conspiracy cases. You are so overwhelmed with the sheer volume of accusations that it is difficult to know where to start to defend yourself. In essence, you don't even recognize 90 percent of where their charges are coming from.

Then they show you the math. Each charge carries a number, many of them representing three points on the sentencing scale. Some only represent one or two, but in the end, to me, it was immaterial. They pile the mound of charges so high that you feel some false sense of relief when you finally get them to say, "OK, we'll drop that one." However, in the mandatory-minimum sentencing procedure, prosecutors have absolutely guaranteed that no one, nor any thing, including the judge, will come between you and a prison sentence. The prosecution holds ALL the cards. The final stake in my heart was their following comment: "We have all the resources of the United States of America at our disposal to prosecute you. We don't know what resources you have, but our guess is they don't match up with ours."

Then, just as I was about to sound my most defiant challenge, they laid these facts on me. The law of conspiracy basically works like this: 1) you are a conspirator if you actually conspired to commit a crime; 2) you are guilty of conspiracy if you were associated with a guilty party, by being a partner or by any other means of association; and 3) you are a conspirator if, BY VIRTUE OF YOUR EXPERIENCE OR FORMAL EDUCATION, YOU SHOULD HAVE KNOWN A CRIME WAS BEING COMMITTED! I was guilty, they said, under the third interpretation. The more I thought about it, I realized they had such a broad blanket with which to bring charges that virtually no one could escape. Ergo, the 99 percent. It is the perfect prosecutorial storm. Think of it this way. A friend or family member tells you he or she got away without paying taxes on unreported income. You are now a conspirator, and depending upon the amount and degree of the accused's action, you could be sentenced to a significant time in federal prison for not turning him or her in. Sound silly? Don't believe it can't and doesn't happen.

This is how the DA's strategy goes when you see an employee subpoenaed, then charged in a case where clearly prosecutors want someone higher in the organization to go to prison. With the law of conspiracy, virtually everyone in an organization who has any interaction with the higher-up individual is completely vulnerable.

The court date was set, and I appeared with the other three defendants, which now included the recently emerged Gary Rose. They each had their own lawyer. It was a rather perfunctory activity. I still couldn't believe this nightmare was happening to me. It wasn't real, was it?

The judge entered all our plea agreements and set sentencing for several months in the future. Just enough time for me to eat my guts out. And the days began to pass, one second at a time.

Before the sentencing, however, there is one more indignity you must endure. You are required to sit down for a presentencing report, where, in my case, a young woman recently out of college sits and writes your life story, **as she hears and interprets it.** This epistle then goes to the prosecuting attorney, then ultimately to the judge. Mind you, this basically is the only document the judge reads regarding your history. In my case, not only did she make several factual errors, but at one point, she even misspelled my name. She made everything I ever did sound dirty. I worked all through high school while playing four sports. Her take: I must have come from a dysfunctional home to have to work like that. I graduated from college. Her take: obviously his education allowed him to be involved in a criminal activity. I was very involved in my church, chairing the finance committee to build a new, $4 million ministry center. Her take: I only was involved to see if I could bilk some of the parishioners (fact, not one was ever approached, nor bought a note in the cattle deal). I built a school for the developmentally disabled and was its head for the first two years of operation. Her take: it was a façade I put on to be accepted into the community. She even said I frequently used an alias—Dick—not stating that this is a standard nickname for Richard, as opposed to an attempt to mislead people as to who I was. Also, you are never allowed to see the document before the judge sees it, so all errors, omissions, and misstatements go against you.

# CHAPTER 22

ONE YEAR LATER, the day of atonement arrived. In a most unusual twist, I was accompanied to the Nashville courtroom by a federal judge from the Western District of North Carolina. He had been a very close friend of mine for years. I coached one of his sons, a very gifted athlete, in soccer, and he coached my son in wrestling. One day, while we were at a state wrestling meeting in Raleigh, North Carolina, I mentioned my indictment to Carl, and the pending sentencing, and he was stunned. "What? I can't believe that," he said. He then asked me for all the facts, and although he could take no professional position in the matter, he would thoroughly review the charges, and go with me to the sentencing as a character witness. After he reviewed the case, he said it was virtually without merit. Unfortunately, he wasn't the judge in the courtroom. He checked with the federal guidelines for a sitting judge to be sure his appearance on my behalf did not violate his code of ethics. He was cleared, and took a day off, paying his own expenses, and accompanied me to Nashville.

When the procedure got under way, and my character references and letters from friends and professionals with whom I had done business had all been presented, the judge asked if there were any others. My friend Carl, the federal judge, then approached the bench, and his credentials were read out loud. The sitting judge smiled and said, "Let the record show that this is the first time in my career as a federal judge that not only has another federal judge come forward as a character witness for a defendant at sentencing, but the visiting judge is the senior judge in this courtroom."

Shortly thereafter, the judge, almost apologetically, said that he had no discretion to go outside the mandatory-minimum sentencing guidelines, and that the prosecution asked for the top of the guidelines, thirty-six months. The judge gave me the bottom, which was twenty-seven months. I asked to be placed in a halfway house, in Charlotte, so that I could continue running a manufacturing business that I had been running the past five years, and that I had ninety employees whose jobs would be jeopardized if I was sent away. The judge approved my request, but added that he had no influence over my placement beyond the recommendation, as that was the purview of the Bureau of Prisons. The bureau, and the bureau alone would make the decision. The judge did give me three months to get my house in order, and I would be hearing where to self-report from the Bureau of Prisons (BOP).

I walked out of that room and said, "Oh my God, I am really going to prison." I was depressed, confused, and couldn't believe what had just happened to me. My life would change virtually 100 percent, into a world I had only knowledge of through television. Abuse, rape, threats, confinement, and total loss of all my basic freedoms. All at one shot. Oh my god!

# CHAPTER 23

THE NEXT NINETY days was pure torture. My attorney had filed an appeal, centered primarily on the fact that I would be assessed a $4 million restitution, which was the same as that imposed on my cattle partner and the two insurance brokers. This not only was completely bogus in my case, since the other three had received all the money, but the amount you are charged with determines the amount of prison time you must serve. To rub salt in the wounds, the two insurance brokers were the only ones who took out a commission for themselves, keeping about $800,000, but as it turned out, the younger one had even cheated his father out of the bulk of the commissions! Apparently, there is no honor among thieves. Worse, as it turned out, the younger one begged the court for mercy, as he had a wife and two small children at home. The father was ill, and his wife was in the hospital with a nervous breakdown. Neither of them went to prison!

I didn't know what to tell my five children, nor most of my friends. By this time, my wife had divorced me, and had the bulk of my assets. My legal bills put me under, financially. Fortunately, I was still the president of a fiberglass firm, and our business was good, so I drew a salary sufficient to survive.

Each day, I waited for word from my Nashville attorney saying that my appeal was being heard, and that a prison term was no longer a forgone conclusion. Tick, tick, tick, the minutes, hours, and days went by, with no word as to the Appellate Court in Cincinnati hearing my case. Note that my attorney did not allow the prosecution to insist on my giving up my rights of appeal as part of the plea agreement. That is a critical strategic step to always take.

I started adding an extra glass of wine at night, which of course compounded the restlessness, and lack of a good night's sleep, which I badly needed.

I had been negotiating with a NASCAR team, as well as one of the big three auto companies, to try out a new quarter-inch nonwoven fiberglass blanket we had developed, with the hopes that their business would substantially escalate ours. Our product was unique, and would significantly reduce the heat inside the vehicle's human compartment, as well as under the hood. All we were doing, businesswise, looked promising.

Finally, I opened my mail on about the eighty-third day, and it was from the Bureau of Prisons, directing me to self-report to the Goldsboro, North Carolina, facility called the Seymour Johnson Federal Prison Camp, which was a six-hour drive from Charlotte. Still, I hoped against hope that my appeal would relieve me of this unconscionable burden. Tick, tick, tick.

The day before my surrender, I met with the owners of the fiberglass company, who had been enormously supportive all this time, and turned the keys over to them. I would pray that the ninety employees would not be likewise punished by losing their jobs after my departure, as the owner was a bright engineer, but had virtually no business acumen. That's why I was hired to build and run the company.

Then I phoned my very, very dear friend, Judge Horn. He told me he wanted to drive me to Goldsboro, which was an incredible gesture. I accepted, and lay in bed that night, never closing my eyes, never moving in the bed.

My third daughter, Christie, came to my rescue in a huge way. After Judge Horn picked me up and whisked me away, she came to my home and took on the huge burden of packing up everything in the three-bedroom house, getting a moving truck, and putting everything in storage. She then took on the additional task of trying to rent it out, and was successful. Thank God for Christie, and her mom.

One more bizarre happening occurred. As it turned out, just making it to prison on time didn't turn out to be a slam dunk. The last night in my home, a hurricane came through North Carolina, destroying roads, trees, homes, and everything in its path. This path just happened to be right between Charlotte and Goldsboro!

Now, here is one more major thing to worry about. We had no idea what the traveling conditions would be on this six-hour journey. Since I was given the right to self-report, instead of being transported all that way in a federal van with wire mesh on the windows, I had to be there ON TIME, which was 2:00 p.m., September 19, 1999. If I was late, the BOP would notify the federal marshals to pick me up, put me in chains, and bring me in any way they could. A hurricane, a frigging hurricane. What's next?

Judge Horn and I discussed everything, except spending time in prison. It was great conversation, talking mostly about our families, our Catholic religion, the economy, and mutual friends. It was refreshing, and took my mind off the inevitable. We did run across many downed power lines, and much debris, but unbelievably, our journey was not interrupted to the point where we could not proceed.

Finally, we reached the small town of Goldsboro. Judge Horn pulled into a restaurant parking lot, and said we were going to enjoy a good lunch together. The term *final meal* was never used. We ate, he paid, and at 1:30 p.m., we headed for the air force base that housed the prison camp. Entering through the guard gate, Judge Horn asked the way to the prison, and the guard showed us the way.

We pulled up in front of the administration building, and we both walked into the reception area. Once I signed in, I turned to my dear friend, we embraced, and I wept. He turned and walked toward the entrance as a prison guard motioned me into an intake room.

"Take off all your clothes, no jewelry, false teeth. What do you have in that bag?" I told him they were my prescription medications that I had been told to bring with me. "Bullshit" he responded, took the bag, and threw it in the trash. "We will decide what medications you take in here." At that, he had me bend over to ensure I wasn't hiding anything in or on my naked body, and provided me with a pair of recently washed boxer shorts, green pants, and a shirt, all of which had been excessively worn, including the underwear, and stunk with an overpowering smell of bleach.

He then handed me my bedding, opened the door to the courtyard, where a dozen or so inmates stood and stared at me, checking me out for God only knew what reason. Finally, after a mug shot, in which I looked like I had not slept in a month, with pale drawn cheeks, I entered what would be my home for an indefinite period of time, with consequences totally and completely unknown.

# CHAPTER 24

I LOOKED AROUND the courtyard, where the dormitories lined both sides of well-manicured grass, and flowers. I was led to my building, Piedmont II, by the intake guard, who opened the heavy metal door and ushered me inside. The lobby was spacious, and had two televisions mounted on opposite sides of the room. No one was in the room, since the inmates were all at their assigned jobs around the camp. Opening the next door led to one of two long hallways, with bunk beds on either side. All beds were made with military preciseness, and the floors were not only clean, but polished so that you could see your image. The beds were all in cubicles, and there were no doors. Six cubes down, and I found my home.

My "cellie," as they referred to themselves, was in the cube, awaiting my arrival. Since he had senior status, his job was to oversee the maintenance of the entire building, so he was always present. He greeted me, and told me the top bunk was mine...same as for all rookies. Within minutes, several other inmates appeared, as if I were the new dog in the park, and they all had to come and have a sniff. "Where are you from, what are you in for, how much time did you get?" I looked around at the men, the climb up to the top bunk (floor, to chair, to top of file cabinet, over the foot rail, into the bed—perfect for a guy with a prostrate problem, who gets up to pee five times a night!).

After living by myself the past five years, the thought of living with seventy-one other men, in one room, sharing one shower, with two washers and dryers, for possibly two and an half years suddenly threw me into the most profound depression I had ever experienced in my life. My throat was burning, my stomach was sick, pressure mounted in my chest, and I asked where the nearest bathroom was. They showed me—down the aisle, turn right, down another aisle, into the tiled area, on your right. I found the six toilets lined up, opened a door, and sat down on top of the seat. I bent over, putting my head in my hands, and absolutely begged God to come to my rescue. Miraculously, literally, within about two minutes, it was like a boil being lanced, or a fever breaking, the fear and panic, and depression disappeared. I returned to my cell, and the men were still standing there.

# CHAPTER 25

MY CELLIE WAS about six feet two inches tall, and was incredibly muscular. He wasn't particularly outgoing, but I soon found out that this was the last two years of a fourteen-year-sentence. He had owned a trucking company, and was caught transporting drugs across state lines, giving him both federal and state sentences.

A Federal Prison Camp, such as this one, was the lowest form of security. The guards, although being omnipresent, carried no guns, but had access to them in the event of an emergency. There was no barbed wire, no fences. Just pine trees surrounding the property. However, escaping was not exactly a piece of cake. We were still on an air force base, where security was extremely tight. Tracking dogs and skilled military personnel seemed to dissuade those who wanted to have a brief roll in the hay with some sweetie. Getting caught leaving the camp also meant they would be sent to a higher-security facility, with substantially reduced privileges, after, that is, they spent ninety days in solitary confinement. During my time at Seymour Johnson FPC, there would be three escapes, and all the absconders were caught and sent to nearby Butner Federal Prison, where such infamous celebs as Bernie Madoff are spending the rest of their lives.

The Camp was basically serving two needs: first, as a reward to men who had much longer sentences, and had good records, and were within the last two years of doing their time; second, for folks like me, white-collar offenders, with sentences under three years, who had no violent offence.

Ostensibly, no one in the camp had a record of violent behavior, at least they had not been convicted of any. However, it didn't take long to figure out how some of my new associates survived the drug wars in the ghettos from whence they came, primarily the DC area, and Florida. Drugs, prostitution, and murder. I never stopped looking at each man with unresolved curiosity.

The Camp had eight dorms, each holding seventy-two inmates. There was a very large dining hall, attached to their rendition of a medical facility, together with the administration building, which housed the warden and his staff. All management, staff, and guards were male, with one exception, a white female tough enough to scare the shit out of a hungry grizzly bear. Some of the staff really, really loved their power. A few, however, were decent.

There was also a maintenance building that housed all the equipment to take care of landscaping, both for the camp, and in areas along the lengthy landing strips, where the F-15 jets took off and landed day and night, with a roar that was staggering. We all had jobs, but the guys I felt for were the ones who had to cut the lawn along these airstrips. Picture this: the location was eastern North Carolina, in the summer. Very hot, very humid. Now add to that the heat thrown off from the jet exhausts and afterburners, which raised the temperature on the pavement to over one thousand degrees. The black men would come back to the dorms purple, and the white men would be so red it looked like they put their faces in a furnace.

Finally, at the other end of the camp was the multipurpose building, where all different denominations held their religious services. Adjacent to that was the law library, and further down a sidewalk was the recreational field, with a track, a basketball court on concrete, and an open-air weight-lifting site. A boccie ball area rounded out the fun-time area.

I had read that many journalists referred to such camps as Club Fed, and talked about the golf courses, tennis courts, and relatively luxurious living. Well, somehow I either missed all that, or those jerks were writing from their home office, and never visited a real camp.

# CHAPTER 26

WITHIN MY FIRST twenty-four hours, I was taught the rules and regulations of how to survive in prison. First and foremost, I had to recognize the actual definition of a prison: "An area where many innocent people are kept, against their will, but nonetheless, willing to accept free food, housing, and clothing for an extended period of time." The education did not come from the manual I was given by the administration when I went in, but by the inmates in the nearby cells.

Rule #1, keep to your own business, as what others do is none of yours; #2, never, under any circumstances, snitch on anyone else, or the "community" would crush you like a bug; #3, there are five showerheads in one, large tiled shower area. Never are there to be more than two men in it at a time, and you'll remain at opposite ends of the shower room; #4, you will wait in line to use the washer and dryer. Never, ever touch another man's clothes, or take them out of a machine; #5, enter another man's cell or cubicle only with the other man's permission, and never when the man is not there; #6, keep your part of your cell absolutely clean, and bed made perfectly, because each dorm got rated each week on the results, and special eating privileges were allotted accordingly. God forbid, you should be the one who screwed up, and the other seventy-one men in your dorm were punished. #6 through #100 would be learned through experience over the next month. But the absolute key was to never do anything that someone else thought showed disrespect. That could be terminal, as I'll describe later.

# CHAPTER 27

ON MY SECOND day at the prison camp, which was a Saturday, when most men didn't have to report to work, I was feeling a little less apprehensive from the guys who had befriended me, so I took a stroll down by the recreation yard. It didn't seem odd to me to see a group of men playing basketball, some walking the track, but a couple perched on a hill appearing as lookouts. Things were relatively quiet, and that's when I noticed two men, by themselves, standing against the fence that surrounded the track. The next thing I knew the bigger one of the two bent the other man over the fence, pulled down his sweatpants, and had his way with him. I couldn't believe my eyes. Shocked would not be an adequate adjective. I was so stunned, I actually got dizzy. I turned around and headed in the opposite direction as fast as I could (walking that is, since running was not allowed in the camp). My God, it REALLY DOES HAPPEN IN THESE PLACES! That was a horrible-enough experience, but that night it was even worse. As I was preparing to go to bed, I looked across the aisle, into the cell directly in front of mine, and…it was the man who had just perpetrated the attack. Now, I thought, I have to sleep on my back for the next two years!

Whether this could be called fortunate for me or not, I later found out that the encounter between the two men was a consensual event, and that all homosexuals were actually housed in their own dorm, primarily for their own protection. The classic finale to this story is that the perpetrator was one of the most frequent attendees at all the religious services.

# CHAPTER 28

THE CULTURE OF the camp was fascinating. There were so many differ-ent personality types, cultures, religions, races, and types of offenses. It didn't take me long to realize that, essentially, this was a "society" like none other. To me, it was like an inverted pyramid. Under normal circumstances in the outside world, the top third of a regular pyramid had the higher income, were better educated, and were more successful folks who generally owned or ran companies, who got elected to public office, who taught in colleges, who were in one way or another key or prominent citizens of their respective communities.

Not here, baby, not here. The entire society, to me, was an inverted pyramid. The "leaders" were the toughest, the heads of the street gangs, the strongest, the street-smart. They continued to intimidate, pull off whatever illegal gambling, and thievery from the kitchen they could, peddle on the black market what goods they procured, and in general, operate at best a microcosm of their former lifestyle. What you observed, you kept to yourself, or else. An interesting element, however, was that there were virtually no direct threats, or fighting. If caught fighting, the inmates were hauled off in chains, put in solitary confinement, and shipped to a higher-security prison, like Butner, frequently with the loss of time off for good behavior. So their activities, when patently illegal, were cleverly clandestine.

One of the first men to befriend me was Bill Aramony, the deposed CEO of United Way. He headed the organization for twenty years, and was convicted of fraud and mismanagement, among other things. Having a girlfriend less than half his age, and secret apartments in the United States and France didn't help his case. He was somewhat famous in the camp because of his high profile.

He invited me to take a walk around the track with him, which was the customary way of speaking about anything either confidential or that related to others incarcerated with us. Initially, it was all questions about me, revealing very little about himself. I had no idea who he was, nor what he was accused of, but he was very bright, and a most interesting person to talk with. I enjoyed his company, at least initially, because the discussions were something above the gutter level we were surrounded with daily. Bill would introduce me to many activities in the camp, and invite me to meetings that ultimately proved very helpful to my surviving the ensuing months.

I met doctors who had cheated on Medicare, and a half dozen lawyers who had dipped into their clients' trust funds and forgot to put the money back. There were a couple of government officials who wound up being on the take, and two police officers (who had to remain anonymous because some of the inmates would literally have killed them if they found out) who were charged with violations of their oath, like enjoying access to the evidence cabinet, particularly when there was cocaine inside. One of the more interesting observations I noted was that in all the time I spent in this prison, I counted twelve different men who had been convicted in conjunction with their wives, and not one of the women, all of whom were charged and convicted too, did one day's worth of time. All twelve women got probation. A coincidence? I don't think so.

Then, there was the whole genre of drug dealers, probation violators, bank robbers (but not with a weapon that was shown), counterfeiters, weapon charges, illegal gunrunners, import/export folks who didn't understand "duty," and many tax evaders, and tax cheats.

But one of the most fascinating people I met was a young black man, with a college education, who was extremely skilled in the computer sciences. He was one of the very few who not only owned up to his crimes, but was very proud of them. He described in detail how he would get the receipt slips after people had put their credit cards through a machine at a checkout counter, then convert that into cash. He would go to a public library where there were computer terminals and access to the Internet and tap into the bank account of the person whose credit card information he had stolen. He had accounts set up at various locations, and would simply transfer the monies into these accounts. He further described with both detail and some glee how he would stay one step ahead of the authorities, since he knew almost to the minute how long it would take law-enforcement officials to track down the location of his computer terminal. "Obviously," I said, "you must have missed it by a minute or two at some time, or you wouldn't be a guest here." He laughed, and said he had that figured out already. When I asked if he was going to go straight, and discontinue this way of life when he got out, he said, "Are you kidding me, and miss all the fun!"

# CHAPTER 29

I REALIZED QUICKLY that I had to figure out a lifestyle, unlike any that I ever conceived of, to make the best of the next couple of years. Learn everything I could about how others survived, what activities were available, how to avoid making a huge mistake, get positioned in the best job I could, and learn new things. Since it took about a month after your initial immersion into the facility before you were put to work, I took the time to lay out a personal itinerary.

First, I decided I would read, and read, and read. I chose three unrelated topics. First, I spent from 6:00 a.m. to 7:00 a.m. reading my Bible in the recreation room, by myself. I studied it hard, took hundreds of pages of notes, and loved every minute of it. Next, I wanted to read difficult writings, to challenge my mind in different ways. I did this in two iterations. First, I went to the law library every day at lunch break, and immediately when work ended, at 3:00 p.m. I read case law, and laws relating to habeas corpus, or illegal imprisonment. (This was helpful when I would assist some of the younger men charged with drug dealing. Often, they were charged with the federal panacea, conspiracy. They would be in a car, and the driver would be caught with cocaine. Because they **should have known**, they, too, received a twelve-to-fourteen-year sentence, which was unconscionable).

I would alternate this reading with classics, history, and philosophy, available in an adjacent room. Finally, each evening, while everyone else watched TV (something I never did one time in all the months of my incarceration—that's where all the arguments and fights broke out), I would read a new novel, one a week, so I could relax before getting my six hours of sleep. It was common for our sleep to be interrupted in the middle of the night by what the BOP called "stand-up counts." We had to jump out of bed and recite our prisoner number to a uniformed officer as he surveyed all those present to ensure no one had escaped that evening.

I received much of my evening reading material from my dear friend, the judge, as well as from a couple of wonderful cousins who made sure I was constantly with interesting material. The books all had to be soft-cover, including my Bible, as the BOP told me folks had in previous years smuggled in all sorts of things, including razor blades, drugs of every description, secret notes, and so forth in the hard-bound covers. Call me naïve once again, but these crooks were good! My golfing buddies purchased subscriptions to the *New Yorker* and the *Wall Street Journal* for my benefit, and kept my sense of humor active by writing of their antics on the golf course from time to time.

Creating a new life for yourself, from scratch, is certainly not unique to me. Many others have done it. But make no mistake about it, when you essentially lose ALL your freedoms at one time, it is suffocating, debilitating, discouraging, and depressing. Your family and friends either become estranged or distant, or a minority stick with you and love you unconditionally. Your freedoms of movement, speech, and free expression, and your right to a hearing, to contact your loved ones whenever you wish, to eat properly, and so on, simply evaporate. When I say your life has changed irrevocably, that is an understatement. It is worse than that. The word "fairness" simply ceases to exist.

Contact with the outside world was extraordinarily limited. Mail call was the one joy of the day, and it came in the evening. We would all line up, and an officer would pull out one letter at a time and read off the name of the prisoner. I had the special benefit of having my sister, Cary, and her best friend, Louise, send me a card every day I was incarcerated. Unbelievable, but true. Also, my best buddy growing up, Jim, and who was my college roommate, owned a small retail store in Michigan, and he would go to the store every Sunday before the store opened for business, and allow me to call him collect, which was the only way you could use the phone. I couldn't wait for Sunday mornings to converse with Jim, and recollect all the great times we had together, plus find out what was going on in the world, unfiltered. Ironically, I received a letter from an old buddy, Roger, whom I hadn't spoken with for almost forty years, and he was now a prosecuting attorney in Phoenix!

The phone system at best was archaic. There were three pay phones, with no booths, so everything the guy next to you was whispering to his wife or girlfriend, you heard, and vice versa. All calls had to be made collect and the BOP outsourced the system to a private firm that charged outlandish rates, then shared a piece of the action with the BOP.

The most serious problem that came, too frequently, from using the phones was the reaction men had once their loved ones told them they were either filing for divorce or leaving them for another man, sometimes a friend of theirs. These men would go crazy. They would become emotionally unstable, particularly since they were completely helpless to do anything about it. The abandonment and rejection were just too much for some, and they wound up going to a medical facility for help, or getting into trouble and being severely disciplined.

# CHAPTER 30

THERE WERE MANY activities available in camp, some of which appealed to me. As well, within the first few months, I decided I would be proactive in several ways. First, Bill Aramony had invited me to join the Toastmaster's Club, the same one where a group gathers and follows an agenda where everyone has the opportunity to give a speech and be critiqued by the others in attendance. There were about fifteen participants, and the meetings were once a week, on Saturday evenings. I always got a kick out of the fact that the BOP required a guard to be in attendance, for what reason I'm still not quite sure.

The group, fortunately, was quite diverse. There were the doctors, lawyers, and business executives, but also we had a few blacks that had no formal training, but wanted to leave the life of street crime behind them. And, of this group, my favorite was a man named David Washington. David was a DC gang leader who once described to me how he got caught. He was up in an apartment, with mail sacks full of hundred-dollar bills. He estimated there was about two hundred thousand dollars in the bags, a two-week haul. When he heard the feds coming up the stairs, he jumped out the window, onto the roof of the police car! Whoops. Gotcha.

David was structured like a Buddha. About five feet, eight inches tall, enormous chest, shoulders, biceps, and thighs. David was training for a world title in what is referred to as a dead lift. That is, picking up a god-awful amount of weight up to your waist, and straightening your back. We almost didn't have enough weights in the weight room, nor room on the barbell, to load up and let him have at it. We were all in awe at the extraordinary strength and power he had.

In any event, David showed interest in trying his hand at public speaking. We could choose our own subjects, but had to adhere to specific guidelines as to the time frame for which we spoke.

The day or evening arrived for David to give his first speech. It was to simply tell the audience about himself, some biographical information that would be of interest to the audience. David had his green prison-issued shirt cleaned, starched, and ironed. He shaved his head all the time, and it was particularly shiny that evening. When it came time for him to speak, he stepped up to the podium, and began to perspire unmercifully. His underarms showed deep rings, and the sweat poured off his bald head. He began to shake uncontrollably. He stood there for what seemed an hour, and finally began to tell his story. He stammered, and stopped and started. His lips quivered. Finally, after about eight minutes, he said that was all he had to say. We all erupted in applause. He was stunned, and began to cry. He told us that that was the hardest thing he had ever done in his life.

David and I became friends after that, and attended some of his religious services together. I'll never forget that the day I was released from prison, he was mopping the floor in the reception room. He came over to me, shook my hand, and handed me a slip of paper. I read it after I got outside. It said, "Please pray for me and my family." In the twelve years since that day, I have never failed to fulfill that promise. David, I hope you are well.

Several of us got together, including Aramony, and put on clinics to those who would be released in the near future. We would help them write résumés and school them on the interview process. This was challenging, since so many had minimal education, and did not exactly speak the King's English. Still, we wanted them to have a better shot at landing a job when they got out, to help reduce the incredible rate of recidivism of 70 percent.

Finally, after being there several months, and hearing all the stories about how 90 percent of these inmates made their (illegal) living, I decided to seek approval to start a new class, entitled "How to Start and Run Your Own Business." The men had never thought about applying for a loan, raising start-up capital, where to locate, what type of business they should start, how to market, how to be competitive, how to price a product or service, and so on. Therefore, I constructed a syllabus, and went to the warden with my idea. He in turn sent me to the head of education (read: GED instructor), and she thought it was a great idea. With final approval, I posted the class, and got an overwhelming response. I limited the class to fifteen at a time and proceeded. I gave them business models, homework assignments, created a case study, broke them up into competing teams, and had them build sample new businesses, and awarded the most comprehensive model built. It was amazing how they responded with a combination of newly acquired rules and guidelines and their innate street smarts. Certificates of completion were given, and generally displayed with pride on the recipient's cell walls. The class turned out to be a real buzz on campus. (One interesting side note: the BOP had planted spies inside the camp. That is, men who were actually on the BOP payroll, but pretended to be inmates so they could integrate themselves and uncover illegal activities. I had one such man in my class, and when I sensed who he was, mysteriously he escaped the next day, never to be heard from again).

# CHAPTER 31

FOR THOSE OF us who entered the prison camp with a specific religious orientation, there would be some challenges ahead. For example, being Catholic in a small southern town, and a prison with about 90 percent blacks, didn't bode well for me. In fact, although the US population is 25 percent Catholic, only seven inmates practiced our religion, out of 572. Frequently, I would receive threatening notes under my pillow, saying that Catholics weren't Christians, and were not welcome (well, hello, I wasn't there voluntarily!). It would have been easy enough to trace the handwritten notes, but to what avail? We were allowed to have Mass once per week, on Wednesday evenings, in the multipurpose building. The prison allowed one local priest to say Mass, but he rarely ever showed up. However, a Eucharistic minister would come and we would have some semblance of a ceremony, and then receive communion. We were not allowed to gather on Sundays, as that day was reserved for others.

The other groups represented included five Jews, about seventy-five Muslims, and one hundred blacks that created their own service, along with an outside pastor, who led the group every Sunday evening. The Jews celebrated on Saturday evenings, and the Muslims on Friday afternoons.

The Muslim group was growing with converts weekly. There were two reasons for this increase. First, they were the only group allowed to meet during the normal work hours, as they had Friday afternoons off.

Secondly, there was a strong air of antigovernment or anti-United States feeling, and since virtually all inmates felt they were unfairly treated in their trials, it was exciting to in essence join a protest group.

The largest group that regularly practiced its religion was the one hundred or so blacks that showed up on both Sunday mornings and Sunday evenings. I would regularly attend the Sunday evening sessions for two reasons. First, since the camp was controlled by the blacks, I wanted to be seen as supporting those who professed to be Christians. I made some very close friends in this group during the prayer meetings. Then, of course, it was the music. Fantastic, old-style southern gospel wailed from the meeting room and could be heard throughout the camp. It was not unusual to have a half dozen guards come into the back of the room, and clap and sing along with the group. The preacher was outstanding. There would be a Gospel reading, and he would preach a sermon based on what had just been read. He saw my white face among the group, and sought me out early in my visits. Subsequently, we had many great talks, and became somewhat close friends. There were three other whites that joined me as well. It was a great learning experience, and exposure to a culture with which I was not totally familiar.

David Washington, mentioned earlier, was a regular attendee at these services and appreciated my support of their conviction. He told me if I ever had trouble with anyone, I should come get him, and it would be taken care of. I was seen frequently walking with him on campus! Unfortunately, one incident occurred when I didn't have the safety of David. Another inmate had decided, for whatever unknown reason, that he didn't want me around. He threatened me one time, and I ignored it. A couple of months later, he followed me into my cube (an absolute no-no) and shouted he was going to kill me. He had a ballpoint pen in his fist, raised to sink into the back of my neck. I turned and confronted him, just as two other inmates walked by. Their appearance surprised my assailant, and he quickly left the building. Had I physically confronted him, we would both be adjudged equally guilty, and would have been sent to solitary confinement, then removed and relocated to a higher-security prison. Since snitching was forbidden by the brotherhood, I had to figure out a way to get this information to the captain of security. Since I was still making name tags, I quickly went and made a new one for him, and when I took it to him, told him the threat on my life. He said I wasn't the first, and he would take care of it. He waited for about an hour after I left, to ensure my confidentiality, then hauled my assailant out in leg irons and handcuffs. To this day, I have no idea what his problem was, but he was somewhat of a loner, and had no close friends.

# CHAPTER 32

WE WERE ALL required to work, five days a week, even those who were infirmed. Work details included landscape maintenance, food service, librarian, housekeeping, and dorm maintenance. When you are first assigned, you are paid $.09 per hour. The interesting thing about this was that everything you wanted to buy in the commissary was full retail. For example, a pair of ordinary tennis shoes would cost about $100. So let's do the math. At $.09 per hour, working forty hours per week, 160 hours per month, it took you 1,111 working hours to buy the shoes… almost. The BOP took out taxes, and any fines the court ordered you to pay. Therefore, you would either need help from home, or ask the judge to give you a life term so you could buy a few necessities each week. I preferred the former, not the latter.

My first job was working in the library, and I soon boned up on the laws of habeas corpus, the right against false imprisonment. Since so many guys came in each day asking someone to help them file these documents, I was determined to do what I could. Many of these inmates were close to being completely illiterate, so exercising their rights under this law was well beyond their capability. A couple of the lawyers who were also now guests of the government, pitched in and assisted them, too. Believe it or not, even though we filed a couple of dozen a month, several got new hearings and ultimately either a new trial, or were released.

There was a copy machine in the library, available for all to use by inserting quarters per copy. Unfortunately, many used the machine to copy gambling chits they used to bet on college football and basketball games. One day, they forgot to take the originals off the top of the machine, and a guard found them. I say unfortunately because the officials assumed I had permitted it, and fired me from the library. For punishment, I was relegated to going on the air force base and cleaning their toilets. Thank God, that only lasted for two days, and I was reassigned to a woodshop, off campus, and on the air base.

About twelve of us worked every day to build the wooden and glass cases that the military used to display folded-up American flags, along with any specific medals a service member may have earned. The man who oversaw the woodshop operation was an outside contractor, and as crooked as they came. He would tell us each Monday how drunk he got over the weekend, whom he screwed, and other sorted details in which we had no interest. One day, he said he had a special project for me. He took me into his office, and pulled out all his paperwork. This included finances and inventory. Soon, he asked me to begin "fudging" the inventory numbers, because we knew he was stealing the BOP blind. When this happened, I went to the administration and simply requested to have a work assignment on the prison campus. (Remember, there were dire consequences for squealing, so I said nothing about why I wanted the transfer). He was super pissed that I deserted him, but I figured it was up to the BOP to find out on its own how much this guy was stealing from the bureau.

I was given the best job in the prison. I became the administrative assistant to the head of all landscaping and equipment. I had a desk, a typewriter, and an office. Part of my duties included learning how to use the machine that made all the name tags for the prison officials. There was actually an art form to be developed, and once I mastered it, I made creative name tags for many of the officials. As soon as one guard would see what I did for someone else, he would come and ask if I could do the same for him. I saved my best, most creative efforts for the warden, and the chief security officer. In the end, this proved to be a very wise choice. I worked at this position until the day I left the facility. (I was informed later by one of the officials with whom I became friends that the head of this facility, to whom I reported, was caught by an unannounced audit dipping into the cash account, and ultimately received a two-year sentence in a federal prison. When even the staff members are crooks, it gets difficult to tell the good guys from the bad guys!)

# CHAPTER 33

THE BIGGEST JOKE (unfortunately) in the prison was the medical care. The physician assigned to keep us well, and to attend to all our medical needs, was a cast-off from Puerto Rico, and headed the facility for many years, until they found out he did not even have a valid medical degree.

When you got sick, you would go to the medical infirmary at 7:00 a.m. when it opened. The attendants took you first come, first served. It was common to have twenty-five people lined up, some coughing, some with diarrhea, others with sores on their skin, or bleeding from a work accident. No problem. Wait your turn.

I had a problem with precancerous lesions on my scalp that a dermatologist had treated for years, and that needed constant freezing. When my scalp became full of sores, I went to see the doctor, and he refused to treat me. Ultimately, I went to the warden, and pleaded not only my case, but for all the others in the camp that needed the same treatment. The next day, the doctor called me into the infirmary, and held up a can of compressed gas that was used to freeze the sores. He said to me: "OK, you wanted me to help you, well here you are," and instead of letting a blast of gas hit my head for a couple of seconds, he held it for about thirty seconds, and had me on the floor begging him to stop. It not only froze the treatment area, but my skull as well. I had a severe headache for hours after that. However, as it turned out, there were almost fifty others who showed up for their delayed treatment. During my stay at the prison camp, three men died of cancer.

When anyone had to go to a nearby hospital for major surgery, the patient was accompanied by a guard, and frequently shackled to the bed. Once the surgery had been completed, and the man was released, he was simply brought to his dorm room, put in his bed, and left unattended. There was never a postsurgical assistant. The man was at the mercy of fellow inmates who took pity on him. When it came time for the patient to eat, one of his nearby cell mates had to go to a guard, get an approval slip to get a meal out of the kitchen, and bring it to the patient. It was barbaric, but somehow it did create a fellowship that would have not occurred otherwise.

To get our prescriptions, we would be notified over a loudspeaker, or a public address system. Your name would be called out for all to hear, and you had five minutes to appear at the window where the infirmary workers dispensed the drugs. Be one minute late, and a guard would be coming after you.

For those who got violently ill during the night, they had to summon a guard, and show their need for immediate medical attention. Still, no physician was ever on duty, so you either warranted an ambulance to the hospital, or had to grin and bear it. We had cases of ruptured appendixes, gall bladder attacks, many high fevers, and a terrible outbreak of flu. The answer: wait in line at 7:00 a.m.

# CHAPTER 34

VISITATION FOR ALL of us was a very, very special occasion. Although there were limited visitations during the week, the primary hours were on the weekends. Families would come and stay in motels in Goldsboro, and be right at the air force guard gate the moment they were allowed to enter. Visitation hours were 9:00 a.m.–3:00 p.m. All visitors had to adhere to the strictest of rules, regarding what they could wear, what they could bring in, whom they could have with them, and be prescreened as to whether they had ever been arrested, and if so for what. A felony in a family member's or a friend's past history automatically eliminated that person from a visit.

The night before visitation was a frenzy of activity in the dorms. Some men who were particularly adept at ironing would make their whole week's pay by making sure their customers' shirts and pants were neatly pressed. Those who were skilled enough to call themselves a barber were very busy until bedtime. (Cutting hair in the dorms was against the rules, but the guards always looked the other way. I had to have another inmate cut my hair, because the prison barbers, who were inmates, too, only knew how to cut the hair of the black inmates, and I wasn't excited to have a special "do.")

I had many visits from friends, family, and loved ones. Sometimes there would be a month or two between anyone coming to see me, but I certainly understood, since it was about a twelve-hour round trip from where most of them lived in Charlotte.

I was blessed by having my oldest daughter, Cindy, and her husband, Jim, visit from out of state. They brought with them my second-oldest daughter, who had severe brain damage at birth, so even though she was in her thirties, she still functioned as a small child. Also, my ex-wife and mother of my four daughters came with them. We had a wonderful visit, and these times were always exciting both the night before their arrival as well as the time you spent together getting up to date with what was happening in their lives. Of course, they were even more anxious to hear how I was getting along. The challenge became not showing the tears that had been welling up in your eyes as they approached the exit door. You knew it would be many months before you would see them again.

I was also blessed by visits from my third daughter, Christie, and my brother came two times. Both times he came, he brought the pastor of our church in Charlotte, Father Richard Bellow. The tone of those discussions was somewhat different from just speaking with your kids. The subject matter tended to be more philosophical, more spiritual, more serious, all of which were appreciated. Also, my cousin Bob and his wife, Barb, drove all the way from Michigan, a round trip of nearly two thousand miles. What a joy it was to see them. The wonderful part of all these visits was there was no judgment. Just love.

One of the most extraordinary visits I received was from my second wife (who had remarried), and the son we had together. He was twelve, and I missed spending time with him terribly. During our divorce process, I was able to have him every weekend, so we played golf every Sunday together for all those years. I was also his soccer coach for eight years, so we spent another three or four days a week together at practice, or going to games. He was my fifth and final child, and together with the absolutely fabulous four daughters I had preceding him, I consider myself one of the most fortunate men/fathers in the world.

This visit was unusual, however, in that the prison camp held an open house one Saturday per year. Prison authorities allowed visitors to enter from 8:00 a.m. until 4:00 p.m., and instead of being confined just to the visitors' hall, they were allowed onto the campus itself, and could view the dorms, dining hall, library, and recreational fields. Special lunches were made by the inmates, and the atmosphere was very festive. My second wife and son were the first ones in line to enter, and the last ones to leave at 3:00 p.m. Our visit was extremely uplifting. Later, I found out that my second wife had a panic attack on the way to the prison, and almost turned around. I was appreciative to her new husband, who encouraged her by phone to continue the journey.

One other visit was special. My attorney from Nashville, Peter, flew all the way to see me, to discuss my appeal. Besides being extremely skilled, he was a saint. He never charged me for 95 percent of his services, primarily because that first lawyer in Charlotte ran off with all my money.

Finally, you could never tell what would go on during one of these family visit times, when all gathered in the one, large visitation room. On the usual weekends, there would be kids everywhere, lots of them screaming, babies with poopy diapers whose odor wafted through the entire room, young and old alike holding hands, some praying together, and on others you could see the unbelievable strain that not having dad or hubby at home was putting on the family. Tears were frequent.

However, you must remember that it is not natural for a man to be locked up without the better things in life, which included, of course, romance. Now there were guards everywhere, keeping a very close eye on what went on. Even though visitors were screened prior to coming in, many were still able to sneak in drugs, cell phones, and money (which was contraband, too).

One day, while the room was packed with families, there was a big commotion in one corner, and the guards went rushing over to see what was going on. To the shock and dismay of some, but the unblemished joy and pleasure of others, the guards pulled back a blanket and there they were, two naked people screwing their brains out! Needless to say, mama was escorted out immediately, and was never allowed to return. Dad was sent to solitary confinement, but it was our understanding he did so with one hell of a big smile on his face. Some things in life apparently are just worth the risk!

# Chapter 35

Whoever set up the food service for the camp must have been a direct relative to the person who was in charge of the quality of medical care we received. The level of expertise/incompetence was clearly visible.

The inmates who did all the food preparation had the best jobs, and they were the ones with the most spending money at all times. Since they had access to all the food, but we were very limited, they would steal the good stuff (say fresh fruits, whole cherry pies, snacks, etc.), then sell them to us in the dorm. While they were working, they would gorge themselves on whatever looked good to them, then put the remnants on our plates for our dining pleasure.

The hamburger was so full of fat that there was a white glaze of grease on top of the meat when served as a main course. Frequently, there were bone chips in the hamburger, because we got the last bit of carving, after the real meat was extricated by a butcher, and he would then scrape the bone for the grand finale.

One of the highlights the prison officials used to show off to visitors was an island in the middle of the dining room that was a hot bar, primarily with three types of beans, along with salad makings. One day, an inmate accidentally bumped into a cart holding the beans du jour, and we saw a pile of rat poop that led up into the food unit. Ugh. End of fine dining from the hot bar.

One of the fellows in the dorm who worked in the kitchen commented on the out-of-date food we were eating on a daily basis. When asked to show us, he brought in several "best used by this date" labels from various food packages, and the winner was one that exceeded that date by—believe it or not—six years!

A precious commodity on campus was bananas. We were allotted one per month, so they turned out to be the official barter unit. Some of the men, like my cellie, would make a wonderful fresh-fruit cocktail once a month. He would get a bucket from his janitor's closet, meticulously clean it, fill it with fresh fruit he conned from those around us, pack it in ice, and serve it to those who contributed their ration of fresh fruit in the past couple of days.

But all was not lost. On Thanksgiving, Christmas, and Easter, the prison camp would spring for all the makings of a feast: turkey, dressing, cranberry sauce, pumpkin and cherry pies, whip cream, mashed potatoes and gravy, sweet potatoes, carrots, peas, and cookies. Wow, we couldn't believe our eyes, and the guys did a great job cooking it all.

During the evenings of each of these events, the dorms would be flush with all the contraband leftovers that the food-service guys would sneak out when their shift ended, and of course offer it for sale to the highest bidder (usually the guys who offered to cut hair for free, or iron clothes for free won the biggest portions of the stolen goodies). In these cases, the guards looked the other way, and we were most appreciative.

# CHAPTER 36

Nearing the end, almost...

The judge had given me twenty-seven months. However, there are a couple of ways to shorten this decreed time. For good behavior, you can get a 15 percent reduction. Also, under certain circumstances, you can get anywhere from one to six months in a halfway house, which is generally much closer to your home and family. In my case, I received a total reduction, calculated as above, of nine and a half months, and was released after seventeen and a half months of incarceration. This was the result of my constantly writing to the BOP in Washington, DC, insisting that my judge had recommended I spend time in a halfway house, not a prison. This was an approved monthly procedure in the event you felt your imprisonment was inappropriate for any reason.

My daughter Christie and my thirteen-year-old son, Connor, were waiting for me to take me to the halfway house, back in Charlotte. The night before leaving prison was the same as the night before I came, sleepless. My heart was racing, and the adrenaline was flowing. The morning I was to leave, I was ushered into an anteroom, and offered a golf shirt in exchange for my prison garb, a pair of cotton pants, and told how and where to sign out. That done, I walked through the same door I had gone through a year and a half earlier. Seeing my daughter and son simply exploded a volume of pent-up emotions in me...all joyous.

My daughter was the same one who had taken care of my home and belongings in my absence. During my period of incarceration, she had gotten pregnant with her first child, and at the six-month mark, had been in a very serious auto accident when a tractor trailer failed to stop in time and crushed her car. Fortunately, the compartment she was in (a Volvo station wagon) was sufficiently intact so that she and her yet-to-be-born daughter survived. She was hospitalized with multiple breaks in her arm, but was otherwise OK. I wasn't notified by prison officials of this serious accident until two days after it happened. This lack of "being there" when my children would most need me played extremely heavy on my heart.

But off we went, with volumes of stories to tell, questions to ask, smiles and hugs lining my way back into civilization. This was a distinct departure from my attitude and emotions upon my arrival many months previously. It became apparent, quickly, that I had some adjusting to do…again. First, even though my daughter was driving 55 mph in a 55-mph zone, I was dizzied by the speed. For a year and a half, the fastest anything had moved was my bowels after eating a pile of greens. It was like I was on a carnival ride, with signposts and other stationary objects flashing by. We stopped for lunch at a fast-food restaurant, and I couldn't believe I had a choice of food, and as much as I wanted. I realized my life was going to come back to me—in-bite size pieces.

Several hours later, when we arrived at the halfway house, the initial exuberance gave way once again to despair. I checked into the facility, which served recovering drug addicts and alcoholics, as well as ex-prisoners of every description. The lobby was dark, dreary, and full of men and women sitting watching TV with gloomy looks on their faces.

I walked up a narrow, creaky stairway, and was shown to my room. Very small, and meant to accommodate two people, there were four beds, double-bunked, and a small closet for all your personal belongings. These four inhabitants shared one bathroom with an adjacent four-bed room, making eight men attempting to agree on who uses what and when. It wasn't always very peaceful.

Surviving the halfway house, I found, had a different set of circumstances than that of prison itself, but not necessarily altogether without significant risks. Now we were back to new rules and regulations, but this time in three categories: the halfway house itself had many very stringent regulations, next the other inmates had their street rules, and finally, I was now under the supervision of the US Probation Office, with very strict compliance issues. While in the halfway house, however, you are still under the direction and control of the BOP, which owns and runs the place. After a while, you are allowed weekend passes to stay with a family member nearby. However, one of their favorite moves was to call you in the middle of the night, and have you drive to the halfway house for a blood test, to ensure you were not indulging in any drugs or alcohol, both still being illegal.

Every inmate, when released from a federal prison, begins serving a probation period, generally three or five years. During this period, you must report to your probation officer at least once a month, in person, and fill out a form indicating what you've done, where you are working, how much you make, and if you've been in contact with any other felons outside the halfway house. This close scrutiny goes on for this entire multiyear period. Further, it is a requirement of both the halfway house and the US Probation Office that you engage in gainful employment ASAP, but no later than within three weeks of leaving the federal facility. This requirement, while very meaningful, was extremely challenging for many of the men as they had few or no employable skills, nor contacts to interview to be hired. Adding to these problems was the fact that most lacked sufficient transportation to a jobsite, and even many lacked decent clothing to both go on an interview and to begin working.

Now, just when you thought you had a decent recovery plan, and that you were primarily out of the proverbial woods, you find out that one critical item seems grossly out of proportion. That is, the repercussions of the law can affect you quite differently from the average citizen. For example, say that a year later, after leaving the halfway house and you are now living with your family, you get stopped for a DUI. In most cases, you would go before a judge, get fined, and if it was the first time, more than likely go home. Not so if you are on probation. The DUI becomes a *probation violation*, and without any courtroom visit, you can be (and usually are) sent right back to the prison where you had done your original time. When I left prison, there were five men who were returned to the facility, and were doing six months' time for just such an infraction.

Therefore, even after exiting your place of incarceration, there are still years of strict rules, regulations, and self-discipline that are mandatory. The problem is that you actually have much more latitude now to get in trouble on a daily basis, because the temptations are everywhere, and the instrument of control rests between your own two ears.

Judge Horn and I decided to try something new with all the men sitting around in the halfway house, subject to being returned to prison because they had not found employment. He was still a sitting judge, so he and I invited several area companies to a meeting at the courthouse. These were companies we thought would have a need for hourly employees, and would give these men a chance. We invited my probation officer to join our efforts, and he enthusiastically did so.

One of the incentives the court system gives to a recently released prisoner is that the authorities will "bond" the person with the new employer to help ensure that if there are any losses due to thievery or related problems, the employer will be covered up to a specified amount. This helped get many men employment. The goal was to reduce recidivism, and we were simply trying to do our part, and it worked.

Here, I was extremely fortunate. My daughter Christie's husband, Mike, was a partner in a Volvo dealership, and he put me to work immediately, structuring a lease-vehicle marketing program. I remain very grateful to him, and to be reengaged in a meaningful vocational effort, and one that paid more than $.09 per hour! However, the government still had its control over my income. I paid 30 percent personal income taxes to the state and federal governments, THEN the halfway house took 40 percent of my gross income during my six-month stay there! Still, 30 cents on the dollar beat the alternative.

# CHAPTER 37

LOOKING BACK, WITH a surprise ending.

From the earliest time when the investigators entered the picture until the final day of my probation, twelve long years had passed. Twelve years of incredible emotional stress, bankruptcies, divorce, broken family, prison, dramatic lifestyle changes, danger, fear, and time lost that will never be retrieved. All ninety employees of the company I was managing (and their respective families) lost their jobs and income, as the company went bankrupt just months before my release from prison.

Most, if not all of this, need not have happened. In retrospect, there are things I would have done differently, and certain recommendations I would make to all who view this personal account. I was greatly honored by my friend, Carl, the federal judge, who was in charge of a seminar at Duke University Law School, and invited me to tell my story. In attendance were federal and state judges, defense attorneys, US district attorneys, and law students from both Duke and Chapel Hill, and the dean of the Duke Law School. After I completed my testimony, I was approached by two assistant district attorneys, who both were incredulous at the entire story. Why? Read the final comments.

Forgive me if some of the following comments seem too simple, routine, and obvious. Lacking a complete awareness of these issues, with all people and circumstances, however, is an assured prelude to serious vulnerability.

- Read and understand the laws of conspiracy, and the other many ways you can purposely or inadvertently fall victim to foul play.
- Know with whom you are associating. If you find the parties cheating on small things, they'll cheat on bigger things as well, if given the opportunity. This is a character trait that you must be conscious and aware of.
- If you observe illegal behavior, even if the suspect is your best friend, advise someone in authority who can take the appropriate action. Believe it or not, you are doing your friend a favor at this time, as the situation may have a local and immediate remedy without major adverse consequences.
- Avoid putting yourself in any situation where you will be subject to compromise.
- And, of vital importance of which I cannot stress too greatly, if you do find yourself in a potentially vulnerable position, and possibly subject to criminal investigation and all the implications that come therefrom, contact a *criminal attorney*, be one 1,000 percent honest with the attorney, and lay out a plan for survival.

Finally, this epilogue. After I was released from prison, out of the halfway house, still under supervision, and trying to get some semblance of my life back together again, I received a call from my attorney in Nashville. He told me that my appeal had finally been heard by the Court of Appeals in Cincinnati, and that…the court overruled the judge in my case, threw out the monetary damages the lower court had assessed against me, and remanded it back to the original court. Same judge, same US attorney, same FBI special agent in the courtroom.

Result: 97 percent of my "exposure" was thrown out—indicating the sentencing was badly flawed. At this level, I should have received only probation, no incarceration. The only money I had received from the cattle debacle was the $150,000 that I had loaned my partner, and that he had paid back. Had my appeal been heard six years earlier, none of this would have happened.

Some punishments, however, continue.

My voting rights were suspended. I cannot own a firearm to protect myself, or even go hunting (the Second Amendment no longer applies). I cannot hold certain jobs. I was refused a volunteer.

position to work with at-risk children, all because the felony "conviction" on my record precludes such acceptance, even though I had been deeply involved with the Guardian Ad Litem program before, and was given a commendation for my service. I am living the "taxation without representation" bitter pill that our forefathers fought so hard against. Once your reputation is besmirched, it is virtually impossible to clear it up.

Thank God for my faith, family, and friends. What else could compare?

Postscript: Additional Managerial Experiences Engaged in By the Author.

Craftsman Graphics: 1982–1984, president.

This was one of the largest commercial-printing companies in the Southeast. Comprised of three divisions: offset one-, two-, and four-color printing, letter press, and direct mailing operations. The company was one of the oldest in the business, and was hemorrhaging money, badly. The owner/founder had simply not kept up with the times.

My "cures" were set forth almost immediately. I closed down the letter press, as it was badly outdated and inefficient. Next, I purchased a miniweb machine, or continuous printing capability that would allow us to engage in an entirely new market, printing annual reports for major corporations. I then opened a New York office to better access the corporate headquarters that we had targeted. Concentrating then on dramatic improvements in all aspects of marketing, hiring, training, and overseeing a whole new effort paid off handsomely.

The result: Within one year the company was very profitable, and was purchased by an Atlanta firm, allowing that company expansion in the eastern United States.

WJAR-TV, Providence, Rhode Island: 1980–1981, VP general manager.

A premier NBC affiliate in the Northeast, the station was struggling to maintain its market share, and was owned by a group of department stores, called the Outlet Company. The department stores were very aged and losing money badly. Fortunately for the senior management of the group, they could cover the store losses with the strong cash flow and profits from the five TV stations and seven radio stations they owned.

The goal was to get the flagship station, WJAR, into the most profitable position possible, showcase it to Wall Street investment banks, and put the entire Outlet Company up for sale.

One of the first acts was to purchase a brand-new syndicated show for our daytime lineup, which was the *Oprah Winfrey Show*. We were one of the first ten stations in the country to take a chance on what appeared to be an up-and-coming new talent.

Concentrating on improving our local news coverage, along with making significant changes in our sales and marketing processes, the management moves began to show results within four months. One interesting side note is about an event that occurred during my two-year tenure. My news director came to me with a special request. He told me he needed approval for a travel voucher for a top reporter, who had found out where a key man was located in the federal government's witness-protection program. He couldn't tell me where the reporter was flying to, but convinced me it was a major story.

I approved the expense, and when the reporter returned three days later, I found out that the information he returned with was directly related to the government's case against the head of the New England Mafia. We went live with the story that night, and the city was stunned. However, not as stunned as we were.

I was sitting in my home after just viewing our eleven o'clock news where the story was repeated from our earlier telecast, and I received a frantic call from my news director. He told me that our news vehicles, parked behind our television studios, had just been blown up, narrowly missing killing members of our news staff, including the reporter who broke the story, when they were exiting the building on their way home. The report was instrumental in sending the Mafia chieftain to prison, where he later died.

With my connections on Wall Street, and the improved performance, the group was sold.

Kasko Enterprises: 1993–1999, president.

Kasko was the only fiberglass recycling company in the United States. It purchased all the unused, waste-textile fiberglass yarn from the only two producers in this country: PPG Industries, and Owens Corning. The company would haul tons of this material into its small facility in north Charlotte each day, run it through a series of chopping, stripping, and drying procedures, then sell it in bulk to firms using it for insulation.

I was introduced to the company chairman by my CPA, who said the chairman/primary owner was an excellent engineer, but not a competent businessman. The company, he said, could be making much more money with the right management.

I was hired as president, and we had a great run. First, I moved the company across town to a much larger, more modern facility. Next, it seemed obvious to me that we could develop an export business, so I put up a website and marketed the material to Europe, immediately getting a major new customer in Milan, Italy.

Finally, I could see all kinds of possibilities with the recycled product if we made it into a finished product. I went about negotiating a buyout of the other shareholders to give the chairman complete control. Together we searched around the Carolinas to find used textile-manufacturing machinery to build a finished product line.

The finished line would produce a quarter-inch-thick, nonwoven blanket that would have many potential uses, and open up new markets for us. For example, samples were given to a NASCAR team to put under the hood, and against the firewall of the race vehicle to dramatically reduce the heat inside, which in turn reduced driver fatigue. Also, Ford Motor Company agreed to try a four-year testing procedure to introduce this blanket material in several places of its vehicles. It was lighter, less expensive, and dramatically more fire- and heat-resistant than the material the company was using.

The years I had with Kasko were great learning, growing, experimenting, and profitable years. Unfortunately, they concluded with my "reassignment" to the federal facility in Goldsboro, as outlined earlier.

Triune Capital: 2006–2008, managing director.

I was hired by this securities firm to completely turn it around. The company had about a dozen stockbrokers, beautiful offices in the center city of Charlotte, and was losing money daily, which meant it was in need of capital.

I found that with the exception of the founder, the management staff was sorely lacking in experience, motivation, and attitude. Some of the brokers were very young and inexperienced, even though they had their required licenses to practice.

The CFO and related staff were the first to go, along with the compliance officer and three other underperforming employees. They were immediately replaced with more seasoned, competent folks. Then the goal was to develop a professional marketing plan, and work one-on-one with the underperforming brokers. Within six months, the company had its first monthly profit.

After a couple of years, I left and moved to Phoenix, where I enjoyed the next three years raising capital for emerging companies, and working directly with them to ensure the funds they had been given were deployed exactly according to the strategic plans they had used when requesting the monies.

And life goes on, albeit with a more cautionary, experienced outlook!

www.ingramcontent.com/pod-product-compliance
Lightning Source LLC
Chambersburg PA
CBHW051321170526
45166CB00002B/632